Friends for Keeps

Friends for Keeps

Building Relationships That Last a Lifetime

/\

Debra White Smith

Beacon Hill Press of Kansas City
Kansas City, Missouri

Copyright 2003
by Debra White Smith

ISBN 083-412-0216

Printed in the
United States of America

Cover Design: Michael Walsh

All Scripture quotations not otherwise designated are from the *Holy Bible, New International Version*® (NIV®). Copyright © 1973, 1978, 1984 by International Bible Society. Used by permission of Zondervan Publishing House. All rights reserved.

Permission to quote from the following additional copyrighted versions of the Bible is acknowledged with appreciation:

The *New American Standard Bible*® (NASB®), © copyright The Lockman Foundation 1960, 1962, 1963, 1968, 1971, 1972, 1973, 1975, 1977, 1995.

The *New King James Version* (NKJV). Copyright © 1979, 1980, 1982 Thomas Nelson, Inc.

Library of Congress Cataloging-in-Publication Data

Smith, Debra White.
  Friends for keeps : building relationships that last a lifetime / Debra White Smith.
     p. cm.
Includes bibliographical references (p.   ).
  ISBN 0-8341-2021-6 (pbk.)
  1. Christian women—Religious life. 2. Female friendship—Religious aspects—Christianity. I. Title.
BV4527 .S624 2003
241'.6762—dc21

2002152576

Contents

Preface   7

1. Golden Friends   9
2. The Ministry of Friendship   17
3. Unlocking the Heart   31
4. Law or Love?   51
5. Surviving Conflict   65
6. The Cycle of Conflict   85
7. Forgiving Friends   101
8. The River of Friendship   113

Notes   125

For my friend, Stacy Steel, who has seen
my dirty house and loves me anyway.

∧∧∧∧∧∧∧∧∧∧∧∧∧∧∧∧∧∧∧∧∧∧∧∧∧∧∧∧∧∧∧∧

A friend loves at all times.
—Prov. 17:17

∧∧∧∧∧∧∧∧∧∧∧∧∧∧∧∧∧∧∧∧∧∧∧∧∧∧∧∧∧∧∧∧

Preface

As with all of my projects, this book is the product of what I have learned through prayerful observation and from the school of hard knocks. Honestly, at one time in my life I struggled in the area of friendships. Indeed, due to issues of deep betrayal and my own inability to trust, I was convinced that I had no true friends; nor did I really want any. Essentially, I viewed friendship as a means to potential heartache. I remember thinking that I had a host of acquaintances but no real friends. What a wretchedly lonely existence! After years of healing, I gradually realized the value of lasting friendships—and that other people would be my friends if I were willing to live Christ, make myself vulnerable, and love even in the face of risking heartache.

After years of living these concepts, I now have many deep friendships. Presently, if you would ask me who my best friend is, I would have to shrug and say, "I have so many different close friends—women and men—I couldn't say which one is my best. They're *all* my best friends! I have 'best writing friends,' 'best church friends,' 'best mom friends,' 'best speaker friends,' and 'best ministry friends.'" Truly, my goal now is to tug every woman who's willing into the circle of my friendship with Christ. Without doubt, when we love Jesus, there is precious little room for withholding our friendship.

But friendships aren't always easy to maintain. I've discovered that most of my friends have flaws, and I'm sure all my friends have discovered that I have a few more flaws than they do! At some point most of my friends have gotten on my nerves, and I *know* I've gotten on their nerves! But I've learned to look past them, as they look past mine, and focus instead on the greater truth of how much we depend on one another for encouragement, love, and support in our walk with God. I've learned not only how to successfully resolve conflict but also how to break free from the cycle of conflict and still embrace those trapped in such destructive patterns.

Wherever you are in your friendship journeys, my hope is that you can learn from my positive choices as well as my horrible mistakes. As you read this book, I pray that you'll remain open to God's voice. If you do, you'll find not only practical tools for building and maintaining intimate friendships but also healing and hope to persevere for our best friend of all—Jesus Christ.

1
Golden Friends

A [woman] who has friends must [herself] be friendly.
—Prov. 18:24, NKJV

When we moved into our current home seven years ago, I learned that an elderly woman lived next door. Because I spent so much time helping my grandmother before she died, I'll always carry with me a deep sense of the loneliness many older people face. So I decided shortly after we settled into our home that I would befriend Edna Earl.

During our first visit I was delighted to meet a gracious, white-haired lady with twinkling brown eyes and a quick wit. Then in her late 80s, Mrs. Earl gave my son, Brett, and me a tour of her home. The main attraction was her various keepsakes from the lives of her sons—then in their 60s. At the time Brett was the ripe old age of one, so I was faced with the task of enjoying my tour while making certain he didn't destroy all our new neighbor's memorabilia.

What started that day was a friendship that stretched for several years. My son and I made a point of going next door to see Mrs. Earl at least once a month and sometimes more often than that. Usually our main objective was to simply sit and listen to her and be available to laugh with her and ask questions about our town "the way it used to be," when she was a young mother.

By the time Brett was three, he was quite adept at

strolling from our yard to Mrs. Earl's. At times we would even do a few odd jobs for her if she requested, and sometimes we would just jump in and take care of a chore that we perceived needed attention.

One day we walked onto Mrs. Earl's dusty back porch and headed toward her door. But Brett stopped and said, "Mama, Mrs. Earl's porch is really dirty. Let's sweep it off."

I was a little tired and was looking forward to sitting and talking—heavy on the sitting. So I said, "No, Sugar—let's go on inside like we planned."

"No, Mama," Brett insisted. "She needs us to help her." He grabbed one of the brooms propped against the wall. "See?" he exclaimed. With a glimmer in his chocolate brown eyes, he started sweeping the back porch.

After a few seconds of watching his chubby legs at work, I was forced to swallow a lump in my throat—a lump that grew from shame. My little boy, with his pure heart and uncluttered mind, had just exhibited Christ's servant heart more than I. Indeed, he showed me the beauty of serving a friend even when you don't feel like it. So I grabbed a broom, and the two of us spent several minutes sweeping the porch. Of course, Mrs. Earl fussed and said we didn't have to do all that, but I knew she was secretly delighted that we cared.

During those few years we enjoyed our friendship with Mrs. Earl, the main thing Brett and I did was simply offer companionship and a listening ear. But by her actions, you would have thought we bequeathed her the rarest jewels every time we stepped in for a visit. Indeed, we offered her something more precious than all the jewels in the world—our golden friendship.

Eventually Mrs. Earl aged into her 90s. And then there came the day when Brett and I were saddened yet honored to attend her funeral. By then Brett was about four and a half, but he fully understood that our friend had gone to be with Jesus. Even though nearly four years have lapsed since Mrs. Earl passed away, and we now have new neighbors, the house next door is still "Mrs. Earl's house." And I'll always remember her den as a place where I had the honor of reliving the past in the eyes of a great lady who was nearly one century old.

> **Kindness is communicating that someone is valuable through our actions.**
> —Gary Smalley
> *Love Is a Decision*

Characteristics of "Golden Friends"

Most people want "golden friends." Indeed, I believe there's a cry from the bottom of our souls for pure friendships that persevere despite circumstances—for people who will embrace us and ask nothing in return. In a world of quick fixes and drive-through windows, it is rare to encounter those who will take the time to actually look us in the eye and listen—and by their very listening say, "You're important. The world may be racing on, but in this moment, you're important to me."

Frankly, at one time I craved those kinds of friendships. But an interesting thing happened over the years. I gradually stopped expecting *other people* to be my golden friends. Instead, *I* started being a golden friend to others. The more I exhibited the traits of a golden friend, the more golden friends I had. Indeed, the woman who embraces her world will find that the world embraces her in return.

If you would like to become a golden friend, ponder the following traits, and begin implementing each of them one at a time in whatever order best suits you. You'll be amazed at how your perspective will change, and the number of people who call you friend will seem to multiply overnight.

A Golden Friend Listens

Here's a great observation from *The Upward Call:* "To be good listeners means that we create space within our hearts to receive the joys and cares of others. Purposefully set aside your need to control and advise, and offer others room to share. Rather than assuming people can learn from us, may we posture our minds to learn from them. The more we hear, the more we will understand and know how to respond."[1]

A Golden Friend Is Loyal

"But Ruth replied, 'Don't urge me to leave you or to turn back from you. Where you go I will go, and where you stay I will stay. Your people will be my people and your God my God. Where you die I will die, and there I will be buried. May the LORD deal with me, be it ever so severely, if anything but death separates you and me'" (Ruth 1:16-17).

A Golden Friend Keeps Her Word

"Jonathan said to David, 'Go in peace, for we have sworn friendship with each other in the name of the LORD, saying, "The LORD is witness between you and me, and between your descendants and my descendants forever"'" (1 Sam. 20:42).

A Golden Friend Encourages

In *Me and My Big Mouth* Joyce Meyer states, "Don't just sit around and wait for somebody to encourage you. And don't refuse to encourage others just because you are not being encouraged yourself. Don't wait for them to come to you, go to them. Remember, the spiritual rule is: you reap what you sow. Right now you may be reaping the fruit of the seeds you have sown in the past by your refusal to encourage others. But that can change. Get busy and sow a new crop!"[2]

A Golden Friend Unconditionally Accepts

Mother Teresa wrote, "When I was in London, I went to see the homeless people where our sisters have a soup kitchen. One man, who was living in a cardboard box, held my hand and said, 'It's been a long time since I felt the warmth of a human hand.'"[3]

A Golden Friend Offers Support Without Judgment

In the words of Joan Anglund, "A bird doesn't sing because he has an answer—he sings because he has a song."[4]

A Golden Friend Applauds Achievements

Mark Twain wrote, "Keep away from people who belittle your ambitions. Small people always do that, but the really great make you feel that you, too, can become great."[5]

A Golden Friend Understands That Everyone Has a Need to Be Loved

"To be manifestly loved, to be openly admired are human needs as basic as breathing," Arthur Gordon said. "Why, then, wanting them so much ourselves, do we deny them so often to others?"[6]

A Golden Friend Makes Individuals a Top Priority

Mother Teresa said, "Every person is Christ for me, and since there is only one Jesus, that person is the only person in the world for me at the moment."[7]

A Golden Friend Recognizes Her Strengths and Utilizes Them

I'm not much on sending cards, but I'm a lean, mean E-mail machine!

Everyone needs golden friends. Even when Christ was on the Cross, He exhibited the human need for friendship.

"Near the cross of Jesus stood his mother, his mother's sister, Mary the wife of Clopas, and Mary Magdalene. When Jesus saw his mother there, and the disciple whom he loved standing nearby, he said to his mother, 'Dear woman, here is your son,' and to the disciple, 'Here is your mother.' From that time on, this disciple took her into his home" (John 19:25-27). As with Christ, friends often fill the gaps left by family members for whatever reason. Friends can be like our sisters, brothers, mothers, fathers, or even sons and daughters. Friendship is certainly a gift from God, intended for our support in the faith and our enjoyment in life.

> **A good heart is better than all the heads in the world.**
> —Edward Bulwer-Lytton

Everyone you encounter every day of your life needs friends as much as you do. Look at everyone as a potential friend. Instead of waiting for other people to be your friend, why not let down the barriers and dare to truly befriend the people who make up the fabric of your life? Ask the mail carrier about his or her grandkids. Encourage the cashier who always checks out your groceries. Have the courage to get really close to the ladies in your Sunday School class.

Many people fall into the groove of choosing a particular type of person for a friend as we might choose a favorite candy bar. But people are living and breathing beings created in the image of God. If we're to live Christ, we must learn to set aside our personal preferences and love people anyway. That's the kind of love Jesus exemplified. His disciples were a diverse group. Nevertheless, He loved each of them.

Just as every person has a different set of fingerprints, enjoying varied friends is like having numerous, distinct fingerprints on our hearts. As human beings, we have many facets to our personalities. Therefore, different friends, with their strengths and weaknesses, are able to complement our differing facets. For instance, I have writer friends, prayer warrior friends, friends who are fellow mothers, older friends, younger friends, and friends with whom I simply enjoy laughing. Realizing that one person can never fulfill every aspect of friendship frees us to develop deep friendships with a variety of people who enrich our lives.

But remember: in order to get into the lives of other people, you'll have to share your life. You'll have to become vulnerable. Therefore, the question remains: whom do I worship: myself or God? If your answer is God, then He will empower you with the courage to be vulnerable for Him. (See chapter 3.)

> **Just as each of us has one body with many members, and these members do not all have the same function, so in Christ we who are many form one body, and each member belongs to all the others. We have different gifts, according to the grace given us.**
> —Rom. 12:4-6

I'm not saying that every woman alive is going to be outgoing and just naturally plunge into a lifestyle of easily making friends. However, even the most reticent of women can bake bread and take it to a neighbor in need. All Mrs. Earl needed was a listening ear and a kind face. Just a smile and a pat on the back are often more than many people receive in a month. You'll soon find that the more you exercise the wisdom of friendship, the easier it becomes. Think in terms of exercising your "friendship muscle." The more you act in friendship, the more you build your abilities to befriend.

Furthermore, it's of monumental importance that we don't turn friendship into an option for only particular personality types. God can and will show you how to use your strengths to create lasting friendships—no matter what type of personality you have. Even the shyest of the shy can learn to give from the heart. And often a shy individual is perceived as a great listener and a wonderful source of strength merely by being there. The more outgoing people will be appreciated for their electric personalities and ability to make people laugh. Whatever your strengths, pledge to use them to the glory of God to create golden friendships that you can cherish and keep for a lifetime.

When we are given our rewards, I prefer to be found to have erred on the side of grace rather than judgment; to have loved too much rather than too little; to have forgiven the undeserving rather than refused forgiveness to that one who deserved it ... to have believed the best and been wrong, than to have believed the worst and been right.
—Gerald Boyer

Think About It

- Ponder this statement by Anais Nin: "Each friend represents a world in us, a world possibly not born until they arrive, and it is only by this meeting that a new world is born."
- Am I limiting my own internal worlds by limiting my friendships?
- Am I as eager to *be* a golden friend as I am to *accept* a golden friend?
- Have I used my personality type as an excuse to avoid taking initiative in developing friendships?
- Make a list of what you want in a friend; then start living that list.

2
The Ministry of Friendship

∿∿∿∿∿∿∿∿∿∿∿∿∿∿∿∿∿∿∿∿∿∿∿

*She gave this name to the LORD who spoke to her:
"You are the God who sees me," for she said,
"I have now seen the One who sees me."*
—Gen. 16:13

The first time I saw her she was walking along the side of the four-lane highway with a toddler struggling at her feet. I was driving home that bright spring day to take advantage of some much-needed writing time. As a committed full-time mom who's also an author, I'm usually running behind on my book deadlines because I don't sacrifice time with my children for my writing. I had just taken the kids to their grandmother's for a visit and was making a straight line to my computer.

Nevertheless, I wasn't so focused on my mission that I missed seeing her—a young mother and her son trudging along the highway. As I neared her, a soft voice within prompted me to pick her up. My head swiveled to follow her progress as I zipped right past her. The inner voice beckoned once again, insisting that I offer her a ride. I glanced in the rearview mirror to see her and her child continuing on their hard journey.

Without another thought, I put on my brake, whipped my Ford Escort into a church driveway, and turned around. Within seconds I pulled up beside her, rolled down my window, and said, "Do you need a ride?"

"Oh, praise the Lord," she breathed. "Yes. Yes, I do! Bless you!" The lithe, beautiful woman secured her chubby-legged son in the backseat and then settled into the front beside me.

"My name is Debra," I said with a warm smile.

"Hi, I'm Cathy." (Name has been changed.) Her attractive, pearly teeth contrasted against her flawless, coffee-colored skin as she bestowed a winning smile on me.

"Where do you need to go?" I asked as the spring sunshine beamed onto the piney east Texas countryside.

"Well, first I was going to the grocery store to get a few groceries. Then I needed to go to the Department of Human Services. And then I was going on to my grandmother's."

As she described the trek she was planning on foot, I calculated that the poor woman had been planning to walk about five miles—and with a two-year-old toddler!

"OK—that's no problem," I assured her, deciding then that the writing would just have to wait.

I gripped the steering wheel and guided the vehicle toward her grocery store of choice. On the way, we chatted a bit, and I soon sensed that Cathy knew Jesus just as I knew Him. Meanwhile, a pianist's rendition of "I Want to Be like Jesus" spilled from my cassette player. Before we got to the grocery store, I sensed the anointing of the Lord all over me. Furthermore, I was so blessed that I was forced to exercise major control to not burst into tears. The only thing that stopped me from a sobbing fit was realizing that my new friend would undoubtedly think she had gotten in the car with a maniac.

The Ministry of Friendship

Within a couple of minutes we were at the grocery store. I offered Cathy some money, but she refused and promised me she had the means for her meager purchases. As she bustled out of the car and got her little boy from the backseat, I continued to listen to my worship cassette. When Cathy shut the back door, the words leaped into my heart, and the tears seeped from the corners of my eyes.

I have one deep, supreme desire—
  That I may be like Jesus.
To this I fervently aspire—
  That I may be like Jesus.
I want my heart His throne to be,
So that a watching world may see
His likeness shining forth in me.
  I want to be like Jesus.

He spent His life in doing good;
  I want to be like Jesus.
In lowly paths of service trod;
  I want to be like Jesus.
He sympathized with hearts distressed,
He spoke the words that cheered and blessed,
He welcomed sinners to His breast.
  I want to be like Jesus.*

—Thomas O. Chisholm

Soon Cathy returned with a couple of bags of groceries —heavily laden with a jug of orange juice and milk. Immediately I wondered how she ever would have made it on the rest of her journey. With my eyes still teary, I cranked the vehicle and began the journey to our next destination —the Department of Human Services.

---

*© 1945. Renewed 1973 by Lillenas Publishing Co. All rights reserved. Used by permission.

On the way, Cathy told me that her husband had left her and her three children and was living with another woman with whom he had a child. He was supplying no support for his wife and kids—ages two, four, and six. Strapped with the responsibilities of young children, Cathy was desperate for some kind of financial aid. And with every word that she spoke, the Lord seemed to whisper, *See why I wanted you to help her? I love her and I need someone to be My hands and My arms and My eyes.*

As we rounded a corner in our small town, Cathy continued to explain that she had just received a negative report from her gynecologist. She was very likely in the early stages of cervical cancer. The desperation in her voice tore at my heart. I tried to imagine the horror of such a report —especially when you're a single mother with three small children. All I could do was keep the tears at bay and offer a sympathetic ear. And that seemed to be exactly what she needed—the listening, and nothing more.

Once we arrived at the Department of Human Services, I agreed to watch her little boy while she took care of her business. Well, the toddler wasn't so keen on that idea. No sooner was his mother out of sight than he started screaming bloody murder from his post in the backseat. Frankly, I probably would have screamed, too, if I had been in his place. He was now dealing with a pale-faced stranger as he watched his beloved mommy enter the brick building.

Before I knew it, I had rounded the car and was scooping him out of the backseat. Like a doting aunt, I gathered him in my arms, held him close, and walked along the sidewalk. With a spring breeze whipping around us, he soon got used to me, and we became fast buddies.

All the while, my watch ticked on. I worriedly bit my bottom lip and calculated the writing time I was sacrificing. Nevertheless, I shrugged and decided that helping my new friend was way more important. After a long absence, Cathy came out of the building with a hopeful report for some financial aid. We tumbled back into the car, and I maneuvered the vehicle toward the parking lot's exit.

That's when Cathy started telling me about her brother. He had been killed in a car wreck six months before, and she was still aching from the loss. He had been a solid Christian who provided emotional support for Cathy, and she was wracked with questions about why the Lord would allow one so kind to be taken from this world. Frankly, I didn't offer her any pat answers or try to sermonize. I just listened and sympathized and told her that I would probably be just as devastated as she was.

As Cathy provided directions to her grandmother's house, a gentle thought nudged at my mind. Long ago I committed my checking account to the Lord. I view that money as God's money, to be used however He chooses. And I knew beyond doubt that He was choosing to use that money that day. A figure of $50 leaped to the front of my mind, and I bestowed an inward nod that Cathy could undoubtedly use that amount.

When I pulled the car into her grandmother's driveway, I whipped out my checkbook and wrote the check. "Take this and use it however you need it," I said.

Her eyes wide, a flabbergasted Cathy took the check and stammered about how no stranger had ever done so much for her. Basking in the glow of the Lord's approval, I also gave her my business card and told her to call if she ever needed me. After Cathy crawled out of my car, retrieved her son and her groceries, and walked into her grandmother's house, I sighed and knew that this was a day I would never forget.

As time has moved on, Cathy and I have maintained a solid friendship. Another friend and I were able to assist her when Cathy underwent a hysterectomy and ultimately received a good prognosis. While she was recovering, I offered to do her laundry a few times. A couple of times I sat in mounds of dirty clothes, dividing them into piles. And the thought occurred to me that this was the essence of the servanthood that Jesus lived.

Since then, I have cheered Cathy on as she has gone back to college and graduated from a computer-oriented program. I've also offered positive references when she applied for jobs. And I've been there for moral support as she has finally decided to take legal action against her unrepentant, adulterous husband. He has now abandoned the other woman and his child by her for a third woman.

Interestingly enough, some time before her surgery, Cathy told my friend that the day I picked her up was the first time anybody had crossed racial lines to help her. What a sadly revealing statement from a 24-year-old Texas woman!

Would you have picked up Cathy that day? I can guarantee that your town has plenty of women just like her. Women in dire straits have been in the world since Genesis. The Bible talks about numerous such women. One of them was Hagar, the servant of Abram's wife, Sarai.

> Now Sarai, Abram's wife, had borne him no children. But she had an Egyptian maidservant named Hagar; so she said to Abram, "The LORD has kept me from having children. Go, sleep with my maidservant; perhaps I can build a family through her." Abram agreed to what Sarai said. So after Abram had been living in Canaan ten years, Sarai his wife took her Egyptian maidservant Hagar and gave her to her husband to be his wife. He slept with Hagar, and she conceived. When she knew she was pregnant, she began to despise her mistress. Then Sarai said to Abram, "You are responsible for the wrong I am suffering. I put my servant in

your arms, and now that she knows she is pregnant, she despises me. May the LORD judge between you and me." "Your servant is in your hands," Abram said. "Do with her whatever you think best." Then Sarai mistreated Hagar; so she fled from her. The angel of the LORD found Hagar near a spring in the desert; it was the spring that is beside the road to Shur. And he said, "Hagar, servant of Sarai, where have you come from, and where are you going?" "I'm running away from my mistress Sarai," she answered. Then the angel of the LORD told her, "Go back to your mistress and submit to her." The angel added, "I will so increase your descendants that they will be too numerous to count." . . .

She gave this name to the LORD who spoke to her: "You are the God who sees me," for she said, "I have now seen the One who sees me" *(Gen. 16:1-10, 13)*.

Hagar's Story

The name "Hagar" is Egyptian and insinuates that Abraham acquired her as a slave when he was in Egypt. Then he gave her to his wife, Sarai, as a handmaiden. In their culture if a wife remained without child, she often arranged a surrogate mother for her husband to impregnate. When Sarai told Abraham to sleep with Hagar, what she suggested was morally wrong and not in God's original plan for marriage. Anytime you see polygamy in the Old Testament, realize that those involved were blatantly living against God's law.

Nevertheless, such marriages were a common practice, even among those who feared the Lord. When the surrogate mother gave birth, the arrangement resulted in the child actually being considered the offspring of the husband and wife, not the husband and handmaid—even though the handmaid was then considered one of the wives. When the child was born, the wife was present during the delivery. The child was then passed to the wife, who held the baby upon her lap. This was a ritual that affirmed that the child really belonged to the wife and her husband, not the servant.

Now even if the plan had been morally right, it was still against God's promise to Abram. God promised Abram that He would multiply his descendants. When time passed and that didn't happen, instead of trusting God's word, Abram and Sarai essentially took matters into their own hands. Anytime we take matters in our own hands, we're asking for problems.

Understand that the person who had authority over Hagar in this story was Sarai, not Abram. When Sarai told Hagar to sleep with Abram, Hagar didn't have a choice in the matter. However, as already mentioned, when Hagar slept with Abram, she essentially became one of his wives rather than a servant. Most servants were delighted to be raised from the servant status to that of wife.

After Hagar conceived, note that her attitude soured, and she developed a nasty attitude toward Sarai. She was arrogant and rude to her former mistress. In turn, Sarai essentially told Abram that the whole thing was *his* fault, despite the fact that the arrangement was Sarai's idea. Then, when Abram told Sarai that Hagar was her handmaiden, he essentially denied any husbandry. In short, he treated Hagar like Cathy's husband treated her when he abandoned her. However, it is important to note that Hagar's attitude wasn't right either. Therefore, they *all* were in the wrong.

From there things went downhill. Sarai didn't just quietly send Hagar away; the scripture says she "mistreated" her. Upon scrutinizing this word in the Hebrew, we learn that Sarai beat her with many stripes, then sent her into the wilderness. I'm surprised that Hagar didn't miscarry. I wouldn't be shocked if Sarai had either taken a few shots at her womb or arranged for that to happen. Hagar, now an unwed mother-to-be, stumbled into the desert and began her trek toward Egypt—most likely back home. Her best-case scenario would have been to make it to Egypt, where as an unwed mother she would have entered society on the lowest rung of the ladder and most likely suffered abuse and neglect. The worst-case scenario was that she would die in the desert.

But instead, she had an encounter with the angel of the Lord. Many noted scholars believe that every time the angel of the Lord appears in the Old Testament he is indeed the preincarnate Christ. From this point of view, Hagar had an encounter with Jesus. He saw her. He heard her. He gave her hope and helped her cope.

> **I am only one, but I am one. I cannot do everything, but I can do something. And that which I can do, by the grace of God, I will do.**
> —Dwight L. Moody

Notice that the angel never once brought up Hagar's wrong attitudes toward Sarai. Was Hagar wrong in scorning Sarai? Absolutely. But the angel of the Lord never said anything like, "Your own bad attitude landed you in this place. If you had just behaved and not gotten all high and mighty with Sarai, she would have never beaten you, and you'd be back where you belong." No, instead the angel simply told her to go back home and submit to Sarai—essentially, to have a cooperative spirit. In other words, the angel *did* address the problem in telling Hagar how to handle the situation exactly at the point at which she messed up in the first place. But the last thing Hagar needed at this point was more beating—whether physical, emotional, or spiritual. So the angel didn't beat her up. Instead, he saw her. He heard her. He gave her hope and helped her cope.

As with my encounter with Cathy, there are times when through us Christ wants to see, hear, give hope, and help others cope. Sometimes the Lord asks us to be His hands, His ears, His mind, and His eyes. He asks us to unconditionally love and befriend those who need help without patronizing or ridiculing them.

But we might think, *I'll love you and be your friend—as soon as I can change you;* or *I'd love you and be your friend if you were of my race;* or *I'll be your friend after I confront you with everything you've done wrong.* But that's not the way Jesus Christ operates. In the New Testament, He embraced all sorts of outcasts who the Jewish leaders would have insisted could never be accepted. And for many of those leaders, even a change in these people wouldn't have made them good enough. Consider the woman caught in adultery, the woman at the well, Zacchaeus, and Judas Iscariot. The woman who was caught in adultery and thrown at Christ's feet wouldn't have been good enough for the Jewish leaders even if she weren't caught in sin. After all, she was a woman, and they believed women were no better than dogs. And no "respectable" Jew would have talked to the Samaritan woman at the well, because they believed their Jewish race was superior to the Samaritan race. Not only were these leaders sexist, but also they were racists. Zacchaeus was a much-hated tax collector; and the name "tax collector" was forever lumped with the term "sinner," someone they wouldn't dare touch because they feared some of the smut would rub off on them. Then there was Judas Iscariot, who ultimately betrayed Jesus and was instrumental in His crucifixion. Even though Jesus knew Judas would betray Him, He still washed Judas's feet. Jesus still loved him.

The Ministry of Friendship

Truly, Christ set aside the prejudices and customs of the day and loved even in the face of being ridiculed. He viewed friendship as a ministry and opened His arms in friendship to anyone who was willing to draw near. According to the authors of *The Upward Call*,

> Most of the people Jesus helped were not friends or relatives. They were strangers of all different backgrounds, ages, and afflictions. Still, each one captured His attention and concern. Strangers may capture our attention, but they rarely evoke enough concern to compel us to service. One reason is that in today's world—with riots, robberies, and drive-by shootings—we are leery of strangers. Why should we try to help someone who may turn around, pull out a gun, and rob us? Television crime coverage has taught us that it is best to lock our doors, hide our valuables, and not get involved.[1]

Within the context of the danger factor, I honestly would *not* have given Cathy a ride if she had been a burly man—unless an angel actually appeared in the passenger seat of my car and instructed me to do so. Since that has never happened in my lifetime, I can assure you I would not have stopped for a man. I don't think it's wise for a woman alone to put herself in jeopardy unless the man is so debilitated that he needs a trip to the emergency room. But in the context of all this, I know many people wouldn't have even stopped for Cathy because they fear getting involved, being taken advantage of, or getting hurt. One of the keys to overcoming such fear is being so in tune with the Lord that you know beyond doubt when He prompts you to act. (See chapter 8.) Because I knew beyond doubt that God told me to help Cathy, I didn't feel even one tremor. I only sensed the anointing of the Holy Spirit from the time I put on my brakes until I dropped her off at her grandmother's.

What would happen in our culture if an army of godly

women decided to release their fears, get involved, embrace the mind of Christ, and view every person they encounter as a potential friend whom the Lord could embrace through them? Have you died to yourself in the area of whom you befriend? In Matt. 16:24 we read these words of Jesus: "If anyone would come after me, he must deny himself and take up his cross and follow me." Essentially, this scripture applies to every area of our lives, including our friendships. Instead of choosing our friends, perhaps it's time for us to ask Jesus whom He wants us to befriend—not in order to change them, but in order to love them and therefore see God miraculously transform their lives from the inside out.

When speaking on the ministry of friendship and resolving conflicts (see chapter 5), I've received differing reports with the same nugget of divine wisdom. One woman told me that the Lord told her to befriend her 18-year-old son. She said that the two of them were at odds and that the Lord whispered that the time had come for her to set it all aside and simply offer love and friendship. Another woman reported that the Lord impressed her to befriend her ex-husband's new wife. She said, "I've been married to him, and I know what his new wife will be forced to go through." Someone else said that the Lord showed her that she was to reconcile with a relative who had pressed false charges against her husband.

And God told me to befriend my own sister, a precious young woman who got on the wrong path in life and wound up at the bottom of a pit. So I befriended her. I stopped acting like the prodigal son's older brother and quit looking down on my sister because of her wrong choices. Instead, I simply embraced her in God's unconditional love and friendship. In my heart I began washing her feet. I therefore watched a divine miracle unfold as she ran into the arms of Christ and began living for Him.

The Ministry of Friendship

Indeed, the ministry of friendship is what the heart of Christ is all about. When we dare to leap into His arms, absorb His unconditional love, and ooze that love on whomever He directs, radical miracles unfold before our very eyes. Whom is the Lord asking you to befriend?

My thoughts are not your thoughts, neither are your ways my ways, declares the Lord. As the heavens are higher than the earth, so are my ways higher than your ways and my thoughts than your thoughts.
--Isa. 55:8-9

Think About It

- Am I asking God to show me people the way He sees them?
- Am I willing to set aside myself and befriend those the Lord calls me to befriend?
- Am I willing to give up some time with my current and comfortable network of girlfriends to spend time in the ministry of friendship?
- Deep in my heart, am I allowing racial, economic, or denominational prejudices to stop me from befriending those Christ wants to embrace through me?
- Am I guilty of being insensitive to the needs of others?

3
Unlocking the Heart

∿∿∿∿∿∿∿∿∿∿∿∿∿∿∿∿

*On the evening of that first day of the week,
when the disciples were together, with the doors locked
for fear of the Jews, Jesus came and stood among them
and said, "Peace be with you!"*
—John 20:19

Memorial Day weekend 2002 was indeed memorable for my family. It all started on Thursday night when a faint, foul odor erupted into a horrific, invisible cloud that burned our eyes and made us gag. I thought my little girl was going to throw up. You see, a skunk decided that our house was a prime target for its complimentary "air freshener." And the thing didn't just spray us once—it sprayed numerous times along the back of our house. We knew we were a multiple-target family, because the scent came in waves. About the time the odious odor would subside, we would suddenly be accosted by another wave.

Of course, I've smelled skunk off and on my whole life, but this was the most direct hit I've ever experienced. I assure you: when you smell a skunk along the highway, that's merely a faint whiff compared to what we experienced. What invaded our nostrils that Thursday night smelled like badly burned rubber, nasty onions, and *skunk!* To say it was *awful* is an understatement.

Nevertheless, my broad-shouldered warrior of a husband went out with a flashlight and walked around the house. Honestly, I wondered what he would do with the thing if he found it. Fortunately, he didn't find it.

The shocking thing is that while we live in a small town, we're still in town. I thought there was some kind of a unstated wildlife law against skunks coming into town. Our neighbor had actually called the dogcatcher on a skunk a few weeks before. I guess we could have called the dogcatcher as well. The way the skunk population seems to be increasing in our town, if I were the dogcatcher I would probably suddenly feel a need to pursue another career.

Meanwhile, we finally settled down for a good night's sleep and hoped the next morning would prove less odorous. Well, it didn't! And guess what—my children had each asked a friend over to spend the night. So my kids and their friends all four awoke Friday morning smelling a little less than pleasant. When we took the friends home, their mothers both commented that they reeked! My son's friend's mom reported that even her child's shoes smelled like skunk!

We spent a couple of days with all the windows open in our home and the fans blowing full-time. My husband and I put our nicest clothes in our vans in hopes that they hadn't absorbed the odor. My daughter's friend's mother said that I might want to check into using the 99-cent cleaners for our clothes. I responded, "Yeah, but do they do skunk?" I could just see myself calling all the cleaners in the area asking, "Do you do skunk?"

Meanwhile, the inside of my purse smelled as if it had been a direct target. For a while when I left the house, I couldn't figure out what about me smelled so bad. Then I realized it was my purse! Even my lipstick cases smelled like skunk.

My pastor's wife, Joy, used one of our hairbrushes to brush her daughter's hair when her daughter visited us Sunday. The next time I saw Joy, she reported that her hand smelled like skunk after using the brush!

Saturday night I called my secretary, Kim Owens. Kim is one of my best friends, and I feel as close to her as if we were sisters. She and I have a wonderful no-nonsense relationship in which we are both completely honest. Along with being one of my dearest friends and my secretary, Kim is the mother of Wesley, the skunk-shoed boy.

I called Kim and said, "The inventory for my on-line bookstore is here in my home office! Do you think all these thousands of dollars worth of books smell like skunk?"

Kim, being the supportive sort, screamed with laughter.

I said, "This is not funny! What am I going to do? When people place their orders on the Internet, I can't ship books that smell like skunk! I guess that if somebody from Europe orders books, they'll get a dose of Texas skunk right along with their books!"

Kim just screamed some more, and her shrill laughter exploded over the line. I imagined by this point she was red-faced and near the point of unconsciousness.

"Look," I said, wondering if she was *ever* going to get a grip. "Do you have a clothesline anywhere? Do you think we could pin some fabric softener sheets between the pages and hang the books on a clothesline?"

More laughter. A lot of help *she* was!

Fortunately, my books weren't affected, and I'm *so* glad! Equally miraculous, our good clothes didn't pick up the odor either! So the 99-cent cleaners were spared! There for a few days every time I saw people I knew, I'd ask, "Do I smell like skunk?" They would sniff in my general direction and say, "No." What a relief!

As I write these words, a month has lapsed since our

skunk fiasco. And we don't smell the odor much as long as we're here. But when we leave and come back home, we encounter that atrocious odor once more!

When my "supportive" secretary came to work shortly after the skunk baptismal, she nearly swooned and said, "I can't work in these conditions!"

I said, "Oh, don't worry about it! You'll get used to it soon, and then you won't even smell it." Sure enough, she became indoctrinated to the aroma of wildlife and stopped noticing the fragrance after a while.

As time goes on, the odor is indeed diminishing. Now we can at least mask the essence of skunk with scented candles. And that's a good thing, for this "visitation" was enough to make us all consider nose amputations!

What's so interesting about foul odors is that, as Kim experienced, at first encounter you think you can't stand it. But then after staying in the ambience awhile, you soon get acclimated to the smell and start thinking everything smells normal. A day or two after the late, great spray, our family had gotten so used to the odor that we actually thought it was gone. Then we left our house. Upon coming back home, we wondered how we could have ever even *imagined* the absence of the odor.

> **When we lose the ability to trust God and others, we die in isolation.**
> —*The Upward Call*

The Fear Factor

Like the skunk smell that engulfed our whole house, fear of intimacy can consume our hearts. Differing situations might cause the initial onset of emotional terror: someone you admired and respected scorns you, an acquaintance betrays you, a best friend dies, or a wicked strand of gossip starts when a friend twists your words. Whatever the situation, the outcome is usually the same—a deep wound that we experience because of friendship gone awry. Soon after the injury, we're usually able to acknowledge that we're engulfed in fear. But after we live with the emotional apprehension for an extended season, we eventually stop recognizing the internal state as abnormal. Indeed, just as our noses grew accustomed to the skunk odor, so our spirits soon grow accustomed to the state of fear. Eventually we come to believe that being emotionally isolated and terrified of close friendships is the norm.

Essentially what many women do is exactly what the disciples did after Jesus' death. John 20:19 says that they had "the doors locked for fear of the Jews." After the trauma of the death of their dearest friend, the disciples did what so many people do after a negative friendship situation: they locked themselves up due to fear. During the writing of this chapter, I received a letter from a woman who read my novel *A Shelter in the Storm*, which deals with a character who constructed walls around his spirit. She wrote,

> *I was so impressed by what you had to say concerning relationships and wall-building in our souls. I have been like many others and have built walls to shut people out of my life so they couldn't have a chance to hurt me by rejecting my friendship. The Lord has revealed to me just how much I do this. I am a reserved person by nature, and so it is a bit difficult for me to start new friendships, even among other Christians in my church. I agree that building walls to keep other people out is also keeping God out of certain areas of my life. I have my comfort zone where I feel safe.*

> **Sometimes I feel isolated,
> so completely alone,
> as if I am entombed
> in a Plexiglass shell.
> I can look out.
> Others can look in.
> But we are separated....
> Some people tell me
> I should not have lonely feelings.
> I should climb out of my shell ...
> as if I can instantaneously
> melt the plastic or will the shell to shatter.**
> —Anonymous

According to C. S. Lewis,

To love at all is to be vulnerable. Love anything, and your heart will certainly be wrung and possibly be broken. If you want to make sure of keeping it intact, you must give your heart to no one.... Wrap it carefully with hobbies and little luxuries; avoid all entanglements; lock it up safe in a casket.... [There] it will not be broken: it will become unbreakable, impenetrable, irredeemable.[1]

While many people fear breaking out of their comfort zones to befriend others, the main fear in interpersonal relationships is often a dread of intimacy. Many are afraid that if they really share and care from their hearts, they will be scorned, disrespected, and criticized. Well, you eventually *will* be scorned, disrespected, and criticized. The more books I write, the more people I love, the more friends I make, the more scorn, disrespect, and criticism I face—sometimes from the very people I thought would always be my friends. Jesus Christ experienced all of that and more; He embraced others anyway. Realize that for every person who criticizes and scorns there will be leagues of others who desperately need a friend and are helped by your openness; the negative people are usually the minority. The question is—are you willing to take the chance on getting hurt in order to further the kingdom of God?

I'm not suggesting that we all enable others to take advantage of us or become masochists who purposefully and foolishly throw ourselves into harm's way. Nor am I saying that we shouldn't allow ourselves room for family and personal time. Realize that Christ often *did* steal away for quiet time or downtime. Everybody needs to be alone some. I have an unlisted phone number; otherwise my phone would ring around the clock. Everybody needs space. However, when we're one-on-one with people and are looking them in the eyes, they know whether we're genuine in our friendship and kind words or if the offer of shallow friendship is a facade behind which we hide.

Frankly, I'm deeply alarmed by people who enforce the fear of intimacy with ministry professionals by telling them to keep a "professional distance" from their congregations. The reason this so alarms me is because during the years that I was trapped in fear of developing intimate friendships, I essentially kept a "professional distance" from many people. On the outside I might have *looked* as if I were enjoying close friendships, but I made a point of holding people at arm's length after a certain point. In turn, I learned that a person reaps what he or she sows (Gal. 6:8). Therefore, I had scores of amiable acquaintances but no truly close friendships. *I believe we've so mistaken amiable acquaintances for true friendships that we've become convinced that shallow relationships are as good as it gets.* Jesus Christ didn't keep a professional distance from the people He was with; He dealt honestly with real issues and embraced the world in love.

One of my main goals as an author and speaker is to follow Christ's example in being real. Therefore, I do my best to deal honestly with real issues and share from my heart. That means that when I step behind a pulpit or podium, talk on television or radio, write at my computer, or interact one-on-one with friends, I'm vulnerable. I essentially don't hide my own struggles as I grow in grace. Rather, I use my own failings and struggles as examples of the pitfalls we all face. In short, I share from the most intimate recesses of my heart—the very thing I was once terrified to do.

Just as sure as the sun daily rises, every time I show myself vulnerable, I get an E-mail from one critical person or another remarking about my "spiritual immaturity." In their estimation, people who have truly arrived don't struggle with issues, aren't sorely tempted, and never miss the mark. Sometimes I hear from someone else who believes that down-to-earth people are really lower by society's standards, and he or she makes a point of doing something to hint at my inferiority. If that isn't bad enough, from time to time I run into people who for one reason or another feel led to remind me of what they believe is their superior stance with God because of gender, denominational affiliation, or pride. Much to my disillusionment, these negative attitudes are at times displayed by those I have tried to befriend. Therefore, in my attempts to be sincere and vulnerable and embrace the world in friendship and love for the cause of Jesus, I've faced numerous demeaning attitudes that the religious leaders in the Bible manifested.

In all due fairness, I must say that the *majority* of men and women I encounter are gracious and thrilled to make a new friend. But when people are trapped in fear of friendship and intimacy, they don't focus on the *majority* of people who will be thrilled with their openness; instead, they focus on those few who will most likely cause them grief. That is exactly what I once did. Because of my fear of being patronized or attacked by the minority, I shut myself off from everyone, including those who might really need my loving friendship. But gradually the Lord began to deliver me from a spirit of fear and encouraged me to open my heart and embrace the world for Him. Indeed, the closer I draw to Him, the less the attacks distract, and the more I'm propelled to love and embrace anyway.

Frankly, many times I've gone home and poured out my pain to my husband because of the attitudes of just those few. Then there have been times when my husband has been as vexed as I while witnessing someone behaving condescendingly toward me. But in these cases I have learned to do exactly what Christ did: expect the negativity as part of life and keep on loving those who need friends. As a result of Christ's love, the vast majority adored Him. Throngs of people followed Him wherever He went. Only a self-centered few were bent upon attack.

If we're going to live Christ in our friendships, then we must be willing to overcome our fear of the minority and embrace the majority. I remember one ministry event in which I poured out my heart and in turn was severely demeaned. When I came home, I was so exasperated that I bluntly told myself I would *never* go back to that church again. Then the Lord reminded me of my commitment to minister wherever He calls even if it involves only *one person* who needs my friendship. Well, there was *one* at that church. I don't know if anybody else got anything out of my visit, but without doubt, that one lady needed an open friend at a crucial point in her life. After the Lord reminded me of my commitment to go, even if for one, I swallowed my words and decided that I would indeed go back to that church and I would be open and vulnerable again—even in the face of being demeaned once more. My commitment to befriend and love people must remain steadfast, regardless of the negative treatment I sometimes encounter.

> I urge you, brothers, in view of God's mercy, to offer your bodies as living sacrifices, holy and pleasing to God—this is your spiritual act of worship. Do not conform any longer to the pattern of this world, but be transformed by the renewing of your mind. Then you will be able to test and approve what God's will is—his good, pleasing and perfect will.
> —Rom. 12:1

Keys to Freedom

A woman who hides her heart behind locked doors eventually locks the door on every relationship, resulting in a lonely existence. Just as Jesus Christ came to the disciples in the locked room and said, "Peace be with you!" (John 20:19), so He can enter our locked hearts and deliver us from fear. Jesus Christ was a man of great passion, love, and vulnerability. The truth is, any woman who dares to radically fling open the door of her heart to Christ and break free of the bondage of fear learns to be vulnerable with the Lord and in turn is willing to become transparent with others.

However, the transition from fear to freedom for some can appear to be an impossibility. But remember Jesus' words: "With man this is impossible, but with God all things are possible" (Matt. 19:26). As you read the following keys to freedom, examine your heart and ask the Lord to begin a miracle of freedom in you today.

> **Our measure of wealth lies in the number of our close friends.**
> —Stan Toler

Unlocking the Heart

First key: Remember that "God has not given us a spirit of fear, but of power and of love and of a sound mind" (2 Tim. 1:7, NKJV). Note the term "spirit of fear." There's a difference between having natural, sensible fears and a *spirit* of fear. Sensible fears might involve not putting ourselves in the path of a tornado, avoiding dark alleys at night, or staying far away from schools of great white sharks. These are healthful, sensible fears that one must possess to survive. A spirit of fear involves living in fear about every corner we turn in life, every relationship we develop. A spirit of fear is exactly what causes us to act like the disciples and hide behind locked doors in our hearts because we *live in fear* of being hurt. Also notice that a spirit of fear is contrasted with love, power, and a sound mind.

Essentially, a spirit of love, power, and a sound mind cannot coexist with a spirit of fear.

> God is love. Whoever lives in love lives in God, and God in him. In this way, love is made complete among us so that we will have confidence on the day of judgment, because in this world we are like him. There is no fear in love. But perfect love drives out fear, because fear has to do with punishment. The one who fears is not made perfect in love. We love because he first loved us. If anyone says, 'I love God,' yet hates his brother, he is a liar. . . . And he has given us this command: Whoever loves God must also love his brother *(1 John 4:16-21)*.

To be free of the spirit of fear,

- Recognize and admit the spirit of fear within your heart.
- Memorize 2 Tim. 1:7, and mentally repeat the verse several times a day.
- During prayer time pray 2 Tim. 1:7 aloud.
- Specifically ask the Lord to begin the healing and deliverance.

- Understand that such deliverance can be instantaneous but most likely will take several months or years as you allow the Lord to walk you through the painful issues that caused you to hide from intimacy.

A faithful friend is the medicine of life.
—Old proverb

Second key: Realize that those who criticize and patronize the loving and vulnerable are criticizing and patronizing everyone they get a chance at. Such scorn is not a personal attack or any kind of honest statement about the one attacked. In other words, most scorners don't choose specific people to dislike or condescend. Rather, they usually wind up criticizing and disliking nearly everyone in their sphere of acquaintances. Habitual censure is a revealing statement about those who attack and means nothing about the person they choose to demean.

I experienced a radical freedom the day I realized that the "religious" people who degraded me for various reasons were also degrading other people for all sorts of other reasons. Indeed, the critical spirit and prejudices are not limited. They are a cancer within the heart of humankind. When a person allows negative attitudes to sprout in one particular area of life, those attitudes have a way of multiplying and taking over the whole heart. For instance, my wise husband says that if someone harbors racial prejudices, he or she will most likely hold gender prejudices as well. I have often witnessed this to be true, because when a prejudice is embraced or a condescending spirit is unleashed, it multiplies a hundredfold and then consumes the heart. As we read in James 1:14-15, "Each one is tempted when, by his own evil desire, he is dragged away and enticed. Then, after desire has conceived, it gives birth to sin; and sin, when it is full-grown, gives birth to death."

A woman who struggles with the fear of being demeaned can find freedom when she

- recognizes that critical people have either few or no *long-term*, healthy friendships;
- understands that nobody can please the one who has allowed prejudices to consume her heart;
- prays that the Lord will give her the spiritual security and freedom not to be devastated by the negative attitudes of others;
- realizes that by recoiling from all friendships because of negative experiences, she has essentially allowed condescending people to put her in their prison;
- accepts that Satan does not want Christians to enjoy freedom in friendships. Therefore, by allowing the fear of being demeaned to consume us, we are empowering Satan's agenda.

> **What have you done today that only a Christian would have done?**
> —Corrie ten Boom
> *Clippings from My Notebook*

Third key: When at all possible, don't respond negatively to negative people. Indeed, "A gentle answer turns away wrath, but a harsh word stirs up anger" (Prov. 15:1). Furthermore, "The tongue that brings healing is a tree of life, but a deceitful tongue crushes the spirit" (v. 4). What usually happens when we respond to negativity in like manner is that the whole ordeal explodes into a nightmare, and the potential for our getting deeply hurt increases tenfold. The deeper we're hurt, the more likely we are to be wrapped in fear. The greater the fear, the greater the spiritual bondage and the greater our chances of never breaking free to enjoy lasting friendships. Just because someone devalues or attacks us doesn't mean we have to defend ourselves. I've learned that a soft word can dissolve censure. Also, when I've been faced with someone who's bent on manifesting a condescending spirit, silence on my part keeps me free to peacefully exit and move on to the next potential friend.

Furthermore, I've learned that if someone is bent on crucifying me anyway, then she'll tear me down even if I rabidly defend myself. Remember that Jesus Christ chose not to verbally defend himself before His crucifixion. They lied about Him. They spit on Him. They hit Him. They flogged Him. "He was oppressed and afflicted, yet he did not open his mouth; he was led like a lamb to the slaughter, and as a sheep before her shearers is silent, so he did not open his mouth" (Isa. 53:7). Then—Christ died for the ones who nailed Him to the Cross. Realize that those who verbally attack, condescend, or criticize are bent upon attack. Self-defense only increases the heat of battle. As the heat of battle increases, so increases the wounds and the difficulty in forgiving.

Furthermore, people who engage in battle against those who attack inevitably inflict wounds upon the attacker. If we're to live Christ, we must be willing to look past negative behavior to the spiritual need of the person who manifests the behavior. When we truly see with Christ's eyes, we then want nothing—not even our own self-defense—to bar the potential for future relationships.

I have recently been involved in a situation in which the Lord has enabled me to minister to someone who indirectly was condescending to me several years ago. Honestly, her judgmental spirit left me simmering for a while, and

I had to work through my aggravation. But in all that, I never once confronted her. If I had heatedly defended myself all those years ago, I would have hurt her and therefore eliminated any chance of befriending and helping her now. Rest assured, I fully understand that there are some situations such as court trials, serious board meetings, and review committees that require us to stand our ground and state facts that might cause pain to others. Nevertheless, the *majority* of life's interpersonal situations usually fall into the category that doesn't demand battle.

Based on all these truths, I have adapted some methods for dealing with censure and criticism. I understand that my life is not yours. Therefore, my circumstances differ from yours. So while you read the following, think of choices you can make to help insure that you won't be shocked into reaction when you're attacked or demeaned. In my life, when the degradation comes in the form of an E-mail, I've learned to hit the delete button unless I'm absolutely required to respond. When negativity comes in a letter, I grimace and drop the offense into the trash if at all possible. When someone tries to attack me over the phone or bad attitudes are manifested one-on-one, I'm learning to ask if I may think about the situation and respond later. Therefore, I have time to meditate, pray, and regain my equilibrium before responding to the situation. As I mention later in chapter 6, one of the things I'm learning to do is ask three simple questions:

- Did you spend 15-20 minutes praying about what you said or wrote before you said or wrote it?
- Did you spend 15-20 minutes praying about it after you said or wrote it?
- Would you be willing to spend 30-40 minutes praying about what you said or wrote before we discuss this any further?

What I am seeing is that most people don't pray about the criticism they slam against others. The ones who agree to pray about it after the fact usually produce an apology. As for the ones who *won't* agree to pray—if they won't take the time to consult God about their negative attitudes, then they certainly aren't going to listen to me. *God* is my defender. As long as I'm seeking Him every day and staying in the center of His will, He is faithful to defend me. Yet if they won't listen to the Lord on my behalf, then my breath is wasted if I try to defend myself.

Furthermore, since I receive so much mail—the great majority of which is positive—I have also asked my secretary to be a buffer for those rare barbs. If she receives negative communication in any form, she doesn't pass on the message unless it earnestly needs attention.

These steps work to keep me grounded in Jesus, free from saying something I'll regret, and protect me from getting so wounded that I revert back to a spirit of fear. As already stated, the more we fight with those who want to wound us, the deeper the battle wounds—on *both* sides. Therefore, there's a powerful freedom in disengaging from a bad situation, resting in the Lord, and responding from His heart of love.

> **Self-Confidence looks inward:**
> **God-Confidence looks upward.**
> —Donna Partow
> *Walking in Total God-Confidence*

Understand that the more honest, open, vulnerable, and willing to embrace others in friendship that we become, the greater a target we are for self-centered people. Therefore, don't be surprised by criticism when you start embracing others in friendship. Instead, be prepared for negativity, and plan how to respond before the attacks happen.

If a woman struggles with how to respond to the barbs that breed the fear of intimate friendships, she may do the following:

- Decide not to be naive. Accept the fact that being free to be vulnerable may cause prideful people to patronize you.

- Develop logical, practical, and biblical methods to deal with the criticism *before* it happens.

- Understand that people who persist in negativity are miserable and in need of friends. Dare to value them so much that you choose not to harm them, in hopes of later ministering to them.

- If at all possible, be willing to quietly learn from criticism. (There have been a few times when I chose to make clarifying adjustments in my ministry efforts due to criticism that initially pricked me but that God ultimately used to show me a need for correction.)

- Memorize and meditate upon the following verses: "A gentle answer turns away wrath, but a harsh word stirs up anger" (Prov. 15:1). "The tongue that brings healing is a tree of life, but a deceitful tongue crushes the spirit" (v. 4).

The moment we "purpose in our heart" to obey Him, at that instant He comes to help us. His incomparable gift is the ability to obey, to move out into what usually looks like uncharted and dangerous country.

—Catherine Marshall
"The Joy of Obedience"

Fourth key: The woman who is free of the fear of intimacy has purposed to base self-worth and inner security upon who she is in Christ rather than peer acceptance or what others think, say, or do.

According to Donna Partow, "Maybe you have a hard time believing that God likes you; maybe you don't even like yourself. But it's true. God not only loves you; he likes you.... Take flight and soar with Total God-Confidence."[2] This kind of confidence with God comes only when we're willing to sit in His presence on a regular basis, as explored in chapter 8. Truly, I've found that the closer I draw to God, the more secure I am in my every relationship. Therefore, if someone chooses to betray me or scorn my offer of friendship, I can run to the bosom of my best friend, Jesus Christ, and find acceptance, love, respect, and a deep sense of being cherished and adored. Despite what any human being ever says or thinks about me, I base my self-worth on the knowledge that the Maker of the universe loves me enough to have died for me.

Once while driving to a women's event where I was scheduled to speak, I was listening to my worship music, basking in the presence of the Lord, and pouring out my praise to Him for His unfathomable anointing. During my torrent of praise, I said something like *O Father, I adore You,* and a thought pierced my prayer—a thought so strong and resounding that I knew I was experiencing a sacred moment: *And do you know how much I adore you?* A shroud of tears cloaked my eyes, and I blinked at the gush of moisture that seeped from the corners. That day I sensed that the Lover of my soul was swelling with as much love for me as I was experiencing for Him.

Understand that no matter where you've been or what you've done, no matter what abuse you've faced at the hands of supposed friends, there is indeed "a friend who sticks closer than a brother" (Prov. 18:24). And He's eager to empower you to break free of the fear of close friendships. Indeed, we're called to learn true intimacy in the arms of the One who created us and then spend a lifetime sharing that intimacy with others. There's no way any of us will ever approach friendship as a ministry or have solid, lasting friendships if we aren't free of fear, wrapped in God's love, immersed in His power, and living the mind of Christ.

If a woman struggles with basing her self-worth upon Christ, she can

- commit several hours a week to radically encountering the Lord;
- imagine the Lord smiling His approval, even when others are less than accepting;
- expect nothing of people except the opportunity to love them;
- when trials come, rest in the Lord, and understand that He will unveil truth in His time;
- memorize the following verse and daily meditate upon it: "I no longer call you servants, because a servant does not know his master's business. Instead, I have called you friends" (John 15:15).

Stars

Yes. I love the stars. I love them.
I love the way they shine for the Hand that created them.
I love their jewel-like magic, diamonds that dreams are made of.
I love their unfathomable number, forever on fire to always inspire.

Yes. I love the stars. I love them.
Come with me. Come with me. We'll fly to the stars.
We'll embrace them and soak up their splendor.
We'll embrace them and blaze with His love.

Yes. I love the stars. I love them.
We are stars. We are stars.
We are the carriers of light. The light of the universe.
We twinkle forth a message the world longs to hear.

He loves you. He loves all.
Come with me. Come with me. Embrace this Giver of Light.
His flame of love will transform dark night.
Yes. I love the stars. I love them.

—Debra White Smith

Think About It

- Am I trapped in the fear of developing close friendships?
- Do I *want* to be free of the fear of close friendships?
- Have I become so accustomed to living in fear of intimacy that I've stopped sensing the fear?
- Have I developed the kind of relationship with Jesus Christ that is teaching me the true meaning of intimacy?
- Do I have the spiritual strength and foundation in Christ that empowers me to base my self-worth on what *He* thinks rather than what others think?

4
Law or Love?

~~~~~~~~~~~~~~~~~~~~~~~~~~~~~~~~~~

He got up from the meal, took off his outer clothing, and wrapped a towel around his waist. After that, he poured water into a basin and began to wash his disciples' feet, drying them with the towel that was wrapped around him.
—John 13:4-5

My friend Janet (name has been changed) went through some dark days as a divorced single mother. During this difficult time she attended a church that she hoped would embrace her in friendship and help her. Initially she was quite impressed. The church people seemed friendly, and the congregation gladly met every Sunday in an impressive million-dollar sanctuary. In the 1970s, that was a top-of-the-line meeting place!

Janet soon began to feel that, according to the views of some of the church members, she was an unacceptable attendee. First, she was divorced. Second, she wore quite a bit of makeup. And third, she was overweight.

More than once, ladies at the church suggested Janet join Weight Watchers. One woman put it even more bluntly, asking why she didn't lose some weight. As Janet reiterated the story, she fought tears of frustration. "Weight loss programs were expensive back then," she said. "I could barely afford to feed my kids, let alone join some program!"

When Janet had surgery, the people of that church did

very little to help her. She was at home with three kids who needed a mother to cook for them. Finally she managed to pull herself into a chair and tell her kids that if they would help her scoot her chair to the stove, she would cook for them. Janet suspected that the reason her church didn't show her more support was because she was divorced.

When Janet's son had surgery, the church folks collected an offering amounting to $200, a good sum 30 years ago. However, when the church representative arrived with the money, he told Janet there would have been more but that some people didn't think the church should give to a divorced woman.

Over the years, Janet has told me this story several times. "They never bothered to find out that my husband abandoned me!" she says. "They just decided that since I was divorced, I was less holy than they were and less valuable!"

Janet's makeup was the third "issue." She remembers the church ladies being more interested in trying to talk her out of wearing cosmetics than helping her provide for her kids. "One day I was cleaning my house and didn't have on any makeup at all," she says. "My hair was pulled up into a bandanna, and I was wearing a T-shirt with a big old bullfrog on the front. The doorbell rang, and there stood one of the ladies who had badgered me about wearing makeup. She took one look at me and my naked face and gasped. I said, 'Now you know why I always wear makeup!'"

Janet's experiences long ago seem out of touch with today's more open-minded culture. But they illustrate the danger that occurs when a preoccupation with rules and regulations overshadows friendship. Thankfully, Janet found another church that wasn't so condemning and has enjoyed long-term fellowship and peace there. But ironically, I have known people in Janet's new denomination who battle similar unloving attitudes.

An overemphasis on rules can cause even the most well intentioned Christians to slip into legalism. The core issue with legalism stems from a wrong heart attitude and results in elevating oneself. Legalism can manifest itself either subtly or blatantly in every denomination and in every person whose focus is law rather than love.

While a message of grace never gives license to sin, so a message of holiness never gives license to legalism.

"People don't experience freedom when we teach legalism," writes Joyce Meyer. "They do experience it when we teach righteousness and freedom from condemnation. Legalism never brings people closer to God. It gets them all tied up in rules and regulations and leaves them no time to fellowship with the Lord [or create new friends]. They are afraid of [God] most of the time."[1]

This sense of condemnation damages our personal relationships with God, Meyer says. It undermines our confidence, steals our joy, and cripples our prayer lives.

Legalistic attitudes can destroy our friendships and ruin our witness. When non-Christians see us as superficial people, they want no part of Jesus. For them, following Christ looks like bondage, not freedom. Try as we might to approach non-Christians in a spirit of friendship, our legalism will cause them to feel condemnation, not unconditional acceptance. Ultimately, a legalistic attitude discourages the most important friendship of all—friendship with Jesus.

A friend of Jesus! O what bliss
That one so vile as I
Should ever have a Friend like this
To lead me to the sky!

> *A Friend when other friendships cease,*
> *A Friend when others fail,*
> *A Friend who gives me joy and peace,*
> *A Friend when foes assail!*
>
> *Friendship with Jesus!*
> *Fellowship divine!*
> *O what blessed, sweet communion!*
> *Jesus is a Friend of mine.*
> —Joseph C. Ludgate

Symptoms of Legalism

I've been in church since I was a child and have heard numerous definitions of legalism. Often these definitions are simplistic and one-dimensional. But legalism is multifaceted. These attitudes happen when we use an outward behavioral standard to determine or assess another's spirituality. This results in a false sense of security as we measure whether or not we're spiritually OK.

If you aren't legalistic but, like Janet, you have been injured by people who are, recognize this cancer for what it is—a falsely spiritual means to elevating the self—and don't fall prey to looking down upon those who are legalistic. This prideful mind-set within itself is legalism as well.

> **Now about brotherly love ... you yourselves have been taught by God to love each other. And in fact, you do love all the brothers throughout Macedonia. Yet we urge you, brothers, to do so much more. Make it your ambition to lead a quiet life, to mind your own business ... so that your daily life may win the respect of outsiders.**
> —1 Thess. 4:9-11

Law or Love?

The following symptoms of legalism are far from simplistic or one-dimensional. I write from experience and from the knowledge of my own delivereance from legalism. As you read, open your heart to the Lord's purging and allow Him to reveal any blatant or subtle traces of legalism within your spirit that would hinder you from developing and maintaining the friendships to which He calls you.

You might be a legalist if . . .

- **You view God as a dictator rather than a God of love.** Legalistic people believe God is looking over their shoulders at every turn, ready to chastise them for every wrong move. Instead of having a grace-based relationship with Jesus, they have a rule-based relationship. They believe that the more rules they can manufacture and keep, the more God will approve of them and the more spiritual they'll become. Ironically, this concept of God and the resulting performance-based relationship with Him creates spiritual pride and stunts spiritual growth. It's a subtle trap! If we begin to view God as a rule-centered dictator, we'll isolate scriptures in order to develop a whole host of rules that our relationships must adhere to. In the church culture, this approach to relationships most blatantly manifests itself in the writings and teachings on marriage. This, of course, creates strictly hierarchical, dysfunctional marriages that are a million miles from God's original design.[2] The dictator view of God also limits the potential to enjoy true friendships. Essentially, no Christian who is truly living by grace wants to be forced into a cookie-cutter mold mentality when it comes to relationships. "He has shown you, O man, what is good. And what does the LORD require of you? To act justly and to love mercy and to walk humbly with your God" (Mic. 6:8).

- **You believe salvation is earned rather than being a free gift of grace.** Many legalistic people believe in salvation by grace. But they unintentionally assess the spiritual depth of other Christians by whether or not they adhere to certain rules that usually have nothing to do with biblical morality. If other Christians don't live by the same set of presubscribed rules, then they are labeled "rebellious Christians" or even "non-Christians." These types of attitudes creep into our lives all too easily. Strangely, some who live salvation by works will cultivate "friendships" with those who don't live by those strict rules. There may be a hidden agenda in place—to reform or change the "worldly" friend. This can cause much hurt when the friend comes to understand that her legalistic friend was really more of a critical acquaintance than a true friend. The friendship is jeopardized, and in some cases the friend is soured on Christianity. "But because of his great love for us, God, who is rich in mercy, made us alive with Christ even when we were dead in transgressions—it is by grace you have been saved . . . in order that in the coming ages he might show the incomparable riches of his grace, expressed in his kindness to us in Christ Jesus. For it is by grace you have been saved, through faith—and this is not from yourselves, it is the gift of God—not by works, so that no one can boast" (Eph. 2:4-5, 7-9).

- **You are in denial about being legalistic.** The first sign that a person is deceived is that she believes she is irrevocably right on all points, has every spiritual issue figured out, and is above deception. Doesn't describe you? Good. But just to be sure, ask yourself if you're experiencing a perpetual discovery of truth and an ever-deepening walk with the Lord. Do you take a rigid approach to Scripture and your relationship with Christ? The Lord regularly shines His light upon areas of our lives that need to be carved into His image. No one has all the answers. If we're not growing spiritually, critical attitudes creep into our lives and we may project a false air of superiority. People who view themselves as superior are not embracing the servant heart of Christ. "In him was life, and that life was the light of men. The light shines in the darkness, but the darkness has not understood it" (John 1:4-5). "This is the verdict: Light has come into the world, but men loved darkness instead of light because their deeds were evil. Everyone who does evil hates the light, and will not come into the light for fear that his deeds will be exposed. But whoever lives by the truth comes into the light, so that it may be seen plainly that what he has done has been done through God" (3:19-21).

- **You use leadership as a means to control.** If a person views God as a dictator, she often condemns others by using scare tactics. She may use the threat of God's displeasure as a manipulation. Undoubtedly, the people who approached Janet probably had been irrevocably convinced that cosmetics were evil. And their own fear-based relationships with the Lord prohibited them from truly befriending Janet as Jesus would. "Do not be called leaders; for One is your Leader, that is, Christ. But the greatest among you shall be your servant. Whoever exalts himself shall be humbled; and whoever humbles himself shall be exalted" (Matt. 23:10-12, NASB).

- **You sacrifice people—their feelings, hearts, well-being —for biblical and/or church rules.** When Jesus healed the man's hand on the Sabbath, the Pharisees were so caught up in their rules regarding keeping the Sabbath holy that they would rather have left the man lame than see him healed. Some church leaders repeatedly choose to condemn those in need and attack sin rather than love people. When we view friendship as a ministry, we never sacrifice people for rules. Instead, we embrace people, as did Christ, and do everything in our power to assist them. My husband, the minister of music at our church, recently spent a whole Sunday helping an ill friend move. This emergency move was a desperate case of move on Sunday or don't move. Our pastor commended Daniel from the pulpit that Sunday morning and said that he was exactly where he should be. Jesus said, "Which is lawful on the Sabbath: to do good or to do evil, to save life or to kill?" (Mark 3:4).

- **You use your own particular denominational doctrine as a platform to demean and look down upon others who hold differing views.** I travel and speak to people of many denominations. There have been times when attitudes were healthier in other denominations than my own, and vice versa. I have encountered legalism in many churches. The attitude manifests itself in every denomination in varying dimensions. Indeed, legalism is a heart problem. I have beloved friends from all walks of the faith, from Catholics to Southern Baptists, from Pentecostals to United Methodists, from Nazarenes to Church of Christ. I have found that in each church there is a remnant of those who are serious about their walk with the Lord, have radically committed their lives to Him, and who in turn are clearly anointed by the Holy Spirit. We are living in the flesh when we disparage people of other denominations. Doctrine and methods of biblical scholarship are extremely important but are never an excuse for snobbery. Those who believe they are superior to others for any reason essentially slam the door in the face of friendship. "'Love the Lord your God with all your heart and with all your soul and with all your strength and with all your mind'; and, 'Love your neighbor as yourself'" (Luke 10:27).

- **You create rules based on isolated scripture and then stand on these rules to look down upon others.** "Persons who read the Word in tiny snippets are far more likely to read their own ideas into scripture."[3] Sometimes these ideas have nothing to do with moral conduct. Rules can be derived from scripture when no verse ever makes a clear statement against one practice or another. Or, if a Bible verse *does* make a statement about the prac-

Law or Love?

tice, legalistic people ignore the spirit of the law in order to enforce the letter of the law. This is what the Pharisees did when they criticized Jesus for healing on the Sabbath. Many people are shocked to learn that Isaac's wife, Rebekah, likely wore a nose ring (see Gen. 24:47, NIV or NASB). Of course, I'm not advocating nose rings. My husband and I don't have them and will never encourage our children to have them. But neither will I condemn or refuse friendship to a person who wears one. Furthermore, I will never believe that a person who wears a nose ring couldn't possibly know Christ. My ears are pierced! Who am I to look down upon or doubt someone's relationship with Christ just because his or her nose is pierced? "Love does no harm to its neighbor. Therefore love is the fulfillment of the law" (Rom. 13:10).

- **You break your own rules and then deny that you're a living contradiction.** I have known people who wouldn't be caught dead in a movie theater watching a movie but would rent the same movie for home viewing or watch it on television. Furthermore, there have been many like the women in Janet's story who scorned others for wearing makeup and then invested hours and major money making certain their hair and wardrobes were perfect, all the while ignoring the fact that the woman scorned for wearing makeup needed food, clothing, medical care, or friendship. Jesus said, "Why do you yourselves transgress the commandment of God for the sake of your tradition? . . . You hypocrites, rightly did Isaiah prophesy of you: 'THIS PEOPLE HONORS ME WITH THEIR LIPS, BUT THEIR HEART IS FAR AWAY FROM ME . . . TEACHING AS DOCTRINES THE PRECEPTS OF MEN'" (Matt. 15:3, 7-9, NASB).

- **You ultimately place self on the throne.** Sometimes we fall into the trap of putting God into our "box" and defining Him by our terms instead of defining *ourselves* in His terms. When we put God into our box and worship our own rules, we're actually worshiping *ourselves* rather than God. Or when we choose to mentally or verbally demean others due to their moral choices, we're still putting ourselves on the throne. "But for the grace of God, there go I" has become a theme of mine. And we who want to live a Christ-centered life are all well served to understand that the only reason we aren't trapped in sin ourselves is because of the love of Jesus. Period. From that healthy mind-set we're free to allow Christ to befriend people through us. Jesus said, "Come to me, all you who are weary and burdened, and I will give you rest. Take my yoke upon you and learn from me, for I am gentle and humble in heart, and you will find rest for your souls. For my yoke is easy and my burden is light" (Matt. 11:28-30).

- **You use Scripture as a means to perpetuate bondage rather than as a means to enlightenment and freedom.** Instead of being free to make friends as the Lord leads, some people place boundaries around themselves and refuse to develop friendships outside their denominational slant or religious group. Do you find yourself avoiding drunken street people, homosexuals, or adulterers? This is not a question of condoning sin. When Christ was confronted with blatant sinners, He showed them mercy and love and invited them to accept His forgiveness. Never did He tell them that their sin was OK or pretend that they weren't in need of forgiveness. But neither did He lambaste, condescend, or refuse to meet their needs. "The teachers of the law and the Pharisees brought in a woman caught in adultery. They made her stand before the group and said to Jesus, 'Teacher, this woman was caught in the act of adultery. In the Law Moses commanded us to stone such women. Now what do you say?' . . . Jesus straightened up and asked her, 'Woman, where are they? Has no one condemned you?' 'No one, sir,' she said. 'Then neither do I condemn you,' Jesus declared. 'Go now and leave your life of sin'" (John 8:3-5, 10-11).

- **You believe that instead of simply being a person's friend and allowing God to grow her, your job is to whip her life into shape.** The legalistic mind-set leads a person to view her own walk with Christ as a onetime or two-time "quick fix" rather than a process of growth in which she spends a lifetime being carved into God's image. When we seriously seek the Lord long enough, we'll eventually come to a point at which He asks us to dedicate our all to Him and become Christ-centered rather than self-centered. However, this doesn't mean we'll ever get to a place at which we're no longer growing in grace. When we start thinking we've arrived spiritually, abundant life is not an option. Beware if you find yourself wanting to fix every problem you see in the other person's life rather than allowing the Lord to enlighten her on the subjects He chooses. If you adopt the "fix it" attitude, your friend will probably break off the relationship because she feels controlled, condemned, and spiritually violated. "The thief does not come except to steal, and to kill, and to destroy. I have come that they may have life, and that they may have it more abundantly" (John 10:10, NKJV).

- **You hang out with legalistic people and support them in their rigid attitudes.** Essentially, legalistic people are limited in their network of close friends because such attitudes result in isolation from God and others. The only people they're comfortable around are people with the same rigid attitudes. Sometimes we fall into the trap of thinking our nonlegalistic friends are under conviction from God because they're essentially "spiritually inferior." We become convinced that when the "spiritually inferior" friend enters the presence of someone who is holy and therefore "spiritually superior," the friend cringes with conviction. In reality, honest conviction from God likely has little to do with our friend's feeling of awkwardness. Rather, the strained relationship is a direct result of the legalist's refusal to love and accept unconditionally. I've known people who would *appear* to have numerous friends, but for the most part these were amiable acquaintances rather than deep friendships. As already mentioned, these relationships eventually dissipate due to the legalistic person's negative attitudes and critical spirit. Jesus said, "I no longer call you servants, because a servant does not know his master's business. Instead, I have called you friends" (John 15:15).

> **Legalism is a religious means to sin.**

When it came to friendship, Jesus Christ didn't examine people's flaws, sins, dress choices, or religious affiliation and then determine whether or not He was going to love them. As a result, the religious leaders criticized Him for mingling with sinners: "He was reclining at the table in his [Levi's] house, and many tax collectors and sinners were dining with Jesus and His disciples; for there were many of them, and they were following Him. When the scribes of the Pharisees saw that He was eating with the sinners and tax collectors, they said to His disciples, 'Why is He eating and drinking with tax collectors and sinners?' And hearing this, Jesus said to them, 'It is not those who are healthy who need a physician but those who are sick; I did not come to call the righteous, but sinners'" (Mark 2:15-17, NASB); "The Son of Man came eating and drinking, and they say, 'Here is a glutton and a drunkard, a friend of tax collectors and 'sinners''" (Matt. 11:19).

Christ opened His arms wide and accepted and loved all people as they were. As a result, thousands and thousands of people followed Him, even out into the wilderness (see Mark 1:45). Obviously, Christ never condoned sin; but He also never condemned the sinner.

Law or Love?

If there was ever a time when people need friends, it's now. If there was ever a time for Christian women to release the legalistic mind-sets and embrace the heart of Christ, it's now. Jesus Christ washed feet to demonstrate His love for the disciples. If we approach friendship as a ministry rather than a rule-based concept, we see each new acquaintance through Christ's eyes. Instead of asking, *What can I get out of this friendship?* or *How can I change you to fit my requirements?* we ask, *What can I give you in this friendship?* or *How can I change myself to better minister to you?* As a result, people who exhibit the heart of Christ soon find they have more close friends than they ever dreamed of. As Gary Smalley put it, "Genuine love is honor put into action regardless of the cost."[4]

> **People don't care how much you know until they know how much you care.**
> —John Maxwell
> *The Power of Thinking Big*

Think About It

- Did I grow up in a legalistic environment?
- If so, how did it affect me?
- Am I legalistic now?
- If so, am I willing to beseech the Lord for forgiveness and deliverance?
- Are there people in my acquaintance whom I haven't befriended due to legalism?

5
Surviving Conflict

∿∿∿∿∿∿∿∿∿∿∿∿∿∿∿∿∿

They had such a sharp disagreement that they parted company. Barnabas took Mark and sailed for Cyprus, but Paul chose Silas and left.
—Acts 15:39-40

East Texas is an interesting combination of the high-tech metropolitan and small towns. In some of these small towns it's almost as if time has stood still. The small east Texas town I live in is no exception. I often jokingly refer to it as Mayberry, USA. However, we *do* have our share of modern problems—such as drugs and alcohol and gangs. We also have our share of modern conveniences—such as Wal-Mart SuperCenter. (Actually, our Wal-Mart SuperCenter is the center of culture for miles around.) But there are some things that haven't changed since 19th-century cowboys drove herds of cattle across the varied Texas terrain.

One night at 3 A.M. my friend Frieda, a single mom, learned just how much the Texas past still affects our small-town present. Frieda awoke to hear a tapping against her window. Being a woman alone, she worried first for the safety of herself and her daughters. Therefore, she stiffened beneath the warmth of her covers and strained to hear any signs of forced entry. Nervously, she peered through the moon-laden darkness to catch sight of any intruder. After several breathless moments, she realized that the invader's attempts to break into her home held a certain cadence. Soon Frieda figured that either the supposed invader had a lot of rhythm, or the tapping entity was not an invader.

After screwing up all her courage, Frieda thrust her feet from beneath the covers, stood up, and walked across the spongy carpet toward the window. She bit her trembling lips, inched aside the curtains, and peered out her window into the darkness. Much to her amazement, Frieda saw something far from a human form. Instead, she encountered a yard full of Texas longhorns. The nearest longhorn stood beside her window, and his tail flapped against the glass with the steady beat of a happy flower-eating beast. The longhorns not only had invaded Frieda's yard but also had stomped into her flower beds and were relishing the rare delicacies.

If you've never seen a Texas longhorn, they're best imagined by starting with a small elephant. In your mind remove the elephant's skin and replace it with white cowhide that has brown spots. Take off the elephant's ears and give it cow ears. Then remove the elephant's tusks and place them near the ears. Elongate the tusks so that they have a six-foot span from one tip to the next. Replace the elephant feet with cattle hooves, and put an obstinate gleam in the creature's eyes. Now you have Texas longhorns! Contrary to popular belief, they're really not cattle —they're "beasts with a moo"!

These beasts with a moo were systematically destroying Frieda's flower beds and leaving hoof marks all over her yard. After several stunned seconds, Frieda dropped the curtain, stood with hands on hips, and determined what exactly to do. Soon she realized she had only one recourse. She did what any other single, independent 21st-century mother would do—she grabbed her phone and dialed 911!

"Hello—please state your emergency."

"Well, uh—I don't know if you could exactly call this an emergency," Frieda hedged. "But you see, I live in town, right across from the high school, and my yard is full of longhorns." Frieda pondered her beautiful flower beds. "And they're eating my flowers!" she wailed.

"OK—we'll send somebody right over," the 911 worker assured.

The good thing about living in a small east Texas town is that the city professionals are probably about the most versatile of any in the nation. Far from considering themselves so specialized that they refuse to perform certain tasks, our police officers are virtual jacks-of-all-trades. They have to be! Who else would save a lady in distress from longhorns at 3 A.M.? True to their word, within mere minutes a police car replete with flashing lights came trolling up the quiet, dark neighborhood. Those cattle, having never seen such a sight, stared in stunned silence. But soon they lowered their ears and trotted right back from whence they had come—across the narrow road, over the school campus, and through the open gate of the neighboring pasture.

Soon after that episode, Frieda learned that the high school agriculture department kept the longhorns in a nearby pasture as a special school project and that "someone" had left the gate open. Believe it or not, "someone" has left the gate open numerous other times since this initial invasion. Now, when Frieda awakens in the wee hours and hears evidence of the mooing, tail-tapping, flower-crunching beasts, she grabs the telephone and dials 911.

"Please state your emergency," the woman always says.

By now Frieda is well known by the emergency crew. She simply says, "Hello, this is Mrs. Scully. The cows are out again." Without asking for further explanation, the dispatcher alerts the policemen.

As usual, the police car comes humming down the street, lights flashing. And by now the cattle are adjusted to the routine. The second they see the revolving lights, they just trot right on back to their pasture like good flower-eating beasts.

Just as the longhorns trample across Frieda's yard, so our friends can sometimes stomp across our lives. It's called conflict. And due to such conflicts we might feel as if our friends were horning their way into our feelings, destroying well-laid plans, and playing havoc with our emotions. Conflicts happen for a variety of reasons. As you read the following list, you might find the reason you have experienced a conflict.

- You're both strong-willed. You may have noticed that most firstborns of their sex in their families of origin have a tendency to be a little too bossy for their own good at times. I'm a strong-willed firstborn, so I speak from experience.

- A close friend says something to you that strikes in a sensitive area.

- There's a part of your heart where you haven't died to yourself and you're unaware of it. So God is using the conflict to reveal your need for growth. The attitude "It's my way or no way" is usually a sign that this problem exists.

- You speak before thinking and offend a friend. The Lord might be using the conflict to teach you to listen for His correction on what you say.

- Physical issues—if you're exhausted, ill, afflicted with chronic pain, or experiencing your monthly cycle, you're much more likely to be snappy.

- Perhaps you or a friend needs to mature emotionally, mentally, or spiritually. A sign of this might be that

Surviving Conflict

you're living in a cycle of conflict. (See chapter 6 for more on the cycle of conflict.)

For whatever reason, conflict happens. I've come to the conclusion that in most conflicts there are three sides: your side, the other person's side, and the right side. Looking back over my life, I must admit that this was the truth with almost every conflict in which I've been involved.

Sadly, many people never realize that they were as much a part of the conflict as the other party, and friendships can even end because of conflicts. Breaking off a friendship because of conflict is like sawing off the limb of a tree because there's a wasps' nest on it. Nevertheless, I have known of friends who stopped speaking to each other for years over a particular conflict.

In short, when friends experience conflict, it should come as no surprise. Conflict is a part of life and should be expected. No matter how spiritually mature two friends might be, they're still human beings and a long way from being perfect. Even such spiritual greats as Paul and Barnabas argued:

> Some time later Paul said to Barnabas, "Let us go back and visit the brothers in all the towns where we preached the word of the Lord and see how they are doing." Barnabas wanted to take John, also called Mark, with them, but Paul did not think it wise to take him, because he had deserted them in Pamphylia and had not continued with them in the work. They had such a sharp disagreement that they parted company. Barnabas took Mark and sailed for Cyprus, but Paul chose Silas and left, commended by the brothers to the grace of the Lord. He went through Syria and Cilicia, strengthening the churches *(Acts 15:36-41)*.

If such spiritual greats experienced a falling-out, how can we deny that the same thing could happen to us? We don't know the outcome, and there's no evidence that either Paul or Barnabas were in a cycle of interpersonal conflict. We'll just say this one dropped in their laps. The question isn't whether or not friendships will experience conflict, but rather, will I choose to resolve my conflicts in a Christlike manner?

While there are varying degrees of and reasons for conflicts, two basic types exist: the onetime conflict that blows up out of nowhere and the cycle of conflict that essentially represents individuals who are lacking mental, spiritual, or emotional maturity. The type of conflict that occurs will determine the method used to resolve the conflict or deal with the other party. While chapter 6 focuses solely upon the cycle of conflict, the rest of this chapter is devoted to presenting the needed tools to resolve the conflicts that seemingly drop into your lap from nowhere.

> **O Father of mercies, grant that I may look on the defects of my neighbor as if they were my own, that I may conceal and be grieved for them; and that making Thy love to us, O blessed Jesus, the pattern of my love to them, I may above all things endeavor to promote their eternal welfare.**
>
> —John Wesley
> *John Wesley's Prayer Manual*

Unbiblical Resolution

I've been in the church my whole life. As a result, I have watched innumerable people fall into conflicts. And frankly, more often than not, I've also observed church people who end their conflicts in a variety of ways, many of which are not scriptural. However, three recurring methods have a way of repeating themselves regardless of location or culture: breaking off the friendship, using the cold-shoulder treatment, and holding a grudge for life.

Breaking Off the Friendship. As previously discussed, some people have a long line of broken friendships in their past. More often than not, this tragedy will occur after a huge verbal blowup when insults are hurled and feelings are trampled. Or it can occur after a series of small tiffs in which one or both parties silently decide to avoid the other. At times this breaking of relationships happens on a larger scale when churches undergo a split.

The Cold Shoulder Treatment. A second way people often deal with conflict is to just stop speaking for a while. Some people may even use this as a method to communicate to the other party that they are angry. Rather than honestly sharing feelings, these people choose to use the silent treatment. Every time you see two such friends locked in silent battle, you can almost hear them growling under their breath, although neither utters a word. Then eventually the newness will wear off the conflict, and both friends will one day act as if all were well. Essentially, what they've done is sweep the issues under the rug rather than resolve the problem. As with marriage, when friends sweep issues under the rug, it leads to eventual heartache, because the problems fester like an untended wound. Eventually the wound might erupt into something akin to a verbal Armageddon, and two friends find themselves thinking something like "I'll never forgive her." This leads us to a third unbiblical method of dealing with conflict: holding a grudge for life.

Holding a Grudge for Life. This tragedy goes beyond merely breaking off the friendship, releasing the past, and moving forward, for deep inside, the grudge-bearer wishes harm upon the other party. Sadly, I've witnessed close friends and/or family members who are still holding a grudge for something that happened 20 years before. Ironically, such attitudes are never isolated to one relationship, because when we harbor unforgiveness, the most important friendship of all suffers—our relationship with Jesus Christ. When our relationship with God suffers, we gradually become more and more self-centered. The more self-centered we become, the more unhealthy all our relationships grow. Eventually, what started as a choice to hold a grudge against one person will spawn a spiritual cancer that spreads its fingers into every relationship we hold dear. Eventually the grudge-bearer might very well find himself or herself participating in a lifestyle of conflict.

> **There are many in the world who are dying for a piece of bread, but there are many more dying for a little love. The poverty in the West is a different kind of poverty—it is not only a poverty of loneliness but also a poverty of spirituality. There's a hunger for love, as there is a hunger for God.**
> —Mother Teresa
> *A Simple Path*

Biblical Resolution

Instead of breaking off the friendship, do everything in your power to repair, rebuild, and to see their side. "Make every effort to live in peace with all men and to be holy; without holiness no one will see the Lord. See to it that no one misses the grace of God and that no bitter root grows up to cause trouble and defile many" (Heb. 12:14-15). When I speak on this subject, I often say that the reason I like verse 14 is because it says that we're to make every effort to live at peace with *all men*; there's no mention of the women! But seriously, this use of the masculine pronoun, of course, involves the entire human race. Aside from the fact that this scripture encourages us to do everything possible to live at peace with each other, it also suggests that when bitterness

Surviving Conflict

sprouts in our hearts, *many* can be defiled. How often that's true of unresolved conflict! When friends are not willing to repair, rebuild, and try to see the other person's side, then those watching—our children, spouse, fellow church members, coworkers—will also be defiled.

When a conflict has occurred, the natural response is to view the whole ordeal through our own viewpoint only. But the mature woman accepts that she is a human being and is not flawless. Therefore, most conflicts are far from one-sided and most likely multidimensional. Few people involved in a conflict remain perfectly Christlike during the whole ordeal. Often emotions rise, wrong attitudes flair, and words are said that are far from loving. Remember: even if you were the one who was initially attacked, if you fell into a heated round of defending yourself in a huffy rage that ultimately led to finger-pointing, the other party wasn't completely to blame for the explosion. She might have started the fire, but an un-Christlike response is essentially like pouring gasoline onto the fire. Keep in mind that when Christ was attacked before His crucifixion, He remained silent. While there's always a time for standing up for what is right, as He did when clearing the Temple, more often than not holding the tongue at the onset of an interpersonal conflict will save feelings as well as friendships. James 1:19-20 states, "Everyone should be quick to listen, slow to speak and slow to become angry, for man's anger does not bring about the righteous life that God desires." Sadly, there are few people who hold their tongue at the onset of a conflict. That's why it's so important when trying to resolve conflict to do our best to see the other person's side.

Recently I realized that someone decided upon meeting me that she disliked me. Her cold behavior toward me at our next meeting confirmed my assumption, as did numerous other encounters when she made it clear that I was simply not her cup of tea. At first I was offended and resentful of her negative behavior. After all, I hadn't done anything to reap her silent censure. But after some time, the Lord showed me that something I said was misunderstood, partly due to her own issues of insecurity. My initial words to her were never intended to be negative. However, in looking at our meeting through her eyes and in light of some of her issues, I'm seeing that perhaps she honestly perceived my comments in a way I never intended. This realization erased the temptation to resent her negative behavior—because I was able to view her through the eyes of Christ. Presently I'm following the Lord and His prompting in handling this particular situation. Initially, He impressed me to remain silent and allow Him to heal the relationship in His time. Recently He began nudging me to offer friendship, and I'm seeing some positive results. While humbly making amends and resolving conflicts are an important element in our walk with the Lord, an equally important element is working in the Spirit and in His time. If I had rushed in under my own power, I would have only created more havoc. (See chapter 6 on dealing with those in a cycle of conflict.) Now I'm seeing the beginnings of what I hope will become a rich and rewarding friendship. Instead of choosing to break off the acquaintance due to our differences, I chose to first see her side and then ultimately repair and rebuild in the Lord's time.

If we are attaching value and honor to the people around us, then we will do our best never to do anything that ties them up in knots. If we do, we will try to untie them.

—Gary Smalley
Love Is a Decision

Instead of sweeping the issue under the rug and pretending all is well, give it a few days, cool off, and then

Surviving Conflict

lovingly approach the person. Eph. 4:15 makes reference to "speaking the truth in love." Verses 31-32 state, "Get rid of all bitterness, rage and anger, brawling and slander, along with every form of malice. Be kind and compassionate to one another, forgiving each other, just as in Christ God forgave you." Within the context of both of these scriptures, understand that this is not a time when you continue the argument. This is about reconciliation—about repairing relationships. Often reconciliation means that the one who was wronged pursues reconciliation, lays down her rights, and does everything in her power to make things right. That's what Jesus Christ did when He died on the Cross for our sins.

According to Gary Smalley, "Biblically, the stronger person always initiates the peace."[1] Therefore, realize that if you're the person who was wronged, then the other party might be spiritually immature. The spiritually mature woman eventually comes to the place that she is willing to lay down her right to be right in order to exemplify God's unconditional love. Often this kind of selfless act will speak the love of Jesus in a way that nothing else can.

Please understand that this is not an exercise in enabling negative conduct. For instance, if the conflict was indeed two-sided, it isn't healthful to take responsibility for the whole ordeal. Such codependent behavior only empowers the other person to continue in her negative patterns. However, you can say, "I'm sorry for my part in our conflict." If the other party stays huffy and isn't interested in reconciling, then learn from previous mistakes and don't "huff" back. Instead, bow out as gracefully, tactfully, and with as much love language as possible. I have actually done this, so I know it's possible with God's help—even for those like me who are at times too quick to speak. Furthermore, a gracious handling of the unrepentant, immature person will enable you to minister to her on the next level of reconciliation, as detailed later in this chapter. And in all this, remember that God is more interested about whether or not we resolve our interpersonal conflicts in a Christlike manner than whether or not we're right.

> **I am fully persuaded that if you had always one or two faithful friends near you who would speak the very truth from their heart and watch over you in love, you would swiftly advance.**
> —John Wesley

Instead of holding a grudge for life, adopt a spirit of forgiveness. A spirit of forgiveness is what I call "preforgiveness." That means, I go into a relationship realizing that my friend or I will eventually say or do something to hurt each other. It's a fact of life, because we're all human. A woman who harbors unforgiveness must also harbor a deep belief that she is better than the other person or above the possibility of sinning. Conversely, a woman who adopts a spirit of forgiveness realizes that she isn't perfect and that she has failed or might eventually fail just as the friend has. Therefore, this wise person decides that with the help of God, she will forgive the other party, no matter what she has done or will do. This is the kind of forgiveness Jesus Christ extended on the Cross. He forgave every sin that had been committed and every sin that was going to be committed. This type of forgiveness is impossible in our own human power; but it's more than possible when we allow Jesus Christ to forgive through us and ultimately impart on us a forgiving spirit. Furthermore, embracing a spirit of forgiveness allows us to build grace-based relationships and frees our friends to be themselves and not feel as if they must walk on eggshells around us. (See chapter 7 for more on this subject as well as hands-on concepts for actually implementing forgiveness.)

> **If you forgive men when they sin against you, your heavenly Father will also forgive you. But if you do not forgive men their sins, your Father will not forgive your sins.**
> —Matt. 6:14-15

The Next Step

I wish life and every person represented a guaranteed set of circumstances and responses. Unfortunately, circumstances and people are as varied as our fingerprints. Therefore, there are always times when you try to implement the above suggestions and your friend isn't interested in making amends. I once experienced such a situation.

The Lord impressed upon me to send a letter of apology to a woman toward whom I had harbored negative feelings. Initially I argued with God with something like "But, Lord, she doesn't know I had a negative attitude toward her." However, the Lord never relinquished the unrelenting conviction that I should somehow try to make peace. At last I determined that the Lord was showing me that He wanted me to write her a letter. So I wrote, asking her to forgive me for my un-Christlike attitude. Shortly after I mailed the letter, I received a scathing letter from her. This came as quite a shock, because I had fully expected her to graciously extend forgiveness and mend our relationship. Instead, she used my apology as a means to elevate herself, look down her nose at me, and rain "fire and brimstone" upon my head. After experiencing her rage, I was eternally grateful that I had listened to the Lord. Indeed, He knew this woman obviously *did* see that I had struggled with a bad attitude toward her. And in His eternal wisdom He understood that I should apologize.

However, now I was in a quandary about what I should do. I debated and deliberated and was tempted to just drop the whole thing. However, my spirit was troubled, and I sensed that the Lord was asking me to respond in love, despite the fact that I was sorely tempted to resent her for life. After a while, I prayed for her and then settled upon buying a nice card from the Christian bookstore. Inside the card I wrote her a friendly note, apologizing once again. I sealed it, put postage on it, and stepped onto my front porch to attach the note to my mailbox with my trusty wooden clothespin (I'm *so* high-tech!). I'll never forget the second I turned from my mailbox to go back into the house. For I was simultaneously struck with a Bible verse and a surge of love that transcended human understanding. The verse was one I had heard my whole life but had seldom applied or seen other Christians apply: "You have heard that it was said, 'You shall love your neighbor and hate your enemy.' But I say to you, love your enemies, bless those who curse you, do good to those who hate you, and pray for those who spitefully use you and persecute you" (Matt. 5:43-44, NKJV).

As I stood at my front door, that supernatural love for the one who blasted me continued to pour through my heart, and the Lord showed me a deep and lasting truth: *while our attitudes do affect our actions, our actions also have a great effect upon our attitudes.* In my situation, instead of struggling with loving this woman from the inside, I *acted* out love on the outside, even though I was tempted to harbor resentment. I prayed for her and for the situation, I did good to her by buying her a special card, and I blessed her in the message that I wrote in the card. In return, the Lord flooded my heart with a love that took my breath away. In

Surviving Conflict

short, if you want to love that person you've been involved in a conflict with, then look at Matt. 5:43-44 as a formula for love: bless her, do good to her, pray for her, and God will fill your heart with a love you can't imagine.

I would love to tell you that the woman in question called me with her apologies or sent a kind note in response. But she didn't. I never heard from her again. Nor did I sense the Lord prompting me to attempt to make any further contact in this particular situation. However, I was *free!* I had asked forgiveness, received censure, and responded in love even in the face of being tempted to harbor ill will. In turn God freed my heart from the bondage of that negative situation and the need for the woman's approval. As already stated, in the real world not everyone responds as we would like them to respond. And frankly, there are some people and situations in which we must do the best we can with God's help and then leave the rest to the Lord.

Remember: complete reconciliation takes *two* parties; and that's the way it works, even with Jesus Christ. Even though God was the one wronged by our sins, He came in the form of a servant, Jesus, and in love died on the Cross for our sins to pursue reconciliation with us. In Luke 15:1-10 Jesus tells of the shepherd who pursues his lost sheep and the woman who searches for her lost coin. So Christ lived out love, opened His arms, and pursued the lost world. However, those who choose *not* to receive Him as Savior find no reconciliation with God. And Christ cannot and will not force himself upon people and demand that they reconcile with Him. Instead, He lovingly approaches and woos each individual and paves the way for reconciliation. If the individual ultimately fails to choose to reconcile with God and closes Him out, then He *remains* out.

Recall the father of the prodigal son in Luke 15:11-32. The son rejected the father, left, and broke the father's heart. Yet the good father never stopped loving his son. Indeed, he threw open his arms of acceptance when the wayward son returned. So we are to exemplify the love of God. When a friend wrongs us, we must be willing to pursue the friend and woo her in love. If the person rejects our efforts, then we must be forever waiting with open arms to freely extend God's love without even a hint of condemnation.

Nevertheless, while the Lord requires us to do good to our enemies, to bless them, to pray for them, and to love them, He never calls us to force them to reconcile. Therefore, if a friend chooses to remain unreachable after you've done everything in your power to fulfill Matt. 5:43-44, then—

- Take peace and comfort in the unconditional love with which the Lord floods your heart.

- Remain available to lovingly pursue reconciliation at a later date as the Lord leads.

- Continue to pray for the estranged friend, and never lose hope that maybe one day the two of you will reconcile.

- In all this, embrace the fact that full reconciliation involves two parties and that you can never do your part in reconciliation and the other person's part too.

If the mainspring of your service is love for Jesus, you can serve men although they treat you as a door-mat.
—Oswald Chambers
My Utmost for His Highest

The Facts of Friendship

The reason I believe this chapter and the next one are so important is because the cavern of conflict is often where we fall in our friendships. Whether we want to admit it or not, conflict happens to good people who have the best of intentions—even spiritual greats like Paul and Barnabas. When you follow Paul through the New Testament, you'll eventually see that Paul changed his mind about Mark—the very person he and Barnabas argued over. Originally, Paul was dead set against including Mark in their ministry. But like us, Paul was a human being who ultimately realized he needed a change in his attitudes toward Mark. Much to Paul's benefit, he didn't allow his differences with Barnabas to end his ministry but rather continued on with the work of the Kingdom and eventually reconciled with Mark.

However, we can become so distracted by who's getting on our nerves that we're no good for the kingdom of God. Matt. 5:13 states, "You are the salt of the earth; but if the salt loses its flavor, how shall it be seasoned? It is then good for nothing but to be thrown out and trampled underfoot by men" (NKJV). Notice that Jesus mentions being salt in the same chapter He talks about doing good to those who spitefully use us.

> **Remaining tender during trial is one of the most powerful ways to build an intimate relationship.**
> —Gary Smalley
> *Love Is a Decision*

In Mark 9:50 we read these words of Jesus: "Salt is good, but if the salt loses its flavor, how will you season it? Have salt in yourselves, and have peace with one another" (NKJV). One of the most powerful ways we can be salt to a world without Christ is by living at peace with one another and doing our best to act out love in the face of scorn. The evil one would like nothing more than to have us at each other's throats so that a watching world will say, "If that's Christianity, I want no part of it." An equally tragic event occurs when we get our focus off Christ and onto conflict. Even if we aren't the ones involved in the conflict, a focus on the conflicts of others will ensure that we slowly begin to drift out of the stream of the Spirit in our hearts and become spiritually stunted.

The Challenge

If you've been involved in any conflicts, whether your friend acted like a Texas longhorn and invaded your yard or you acted like a longhorn yourself, go to your prayer spot and ask God to show you what you need to do to make amends. Wait on Him—even if it takes several hours over a course of several weeks—and then act on what He shows you.

> **A difficult crisis can be more readily endured if we retain the conviction that our existence holds a purpose— a cause to pursue, a person to love, a goal to achieve.**
> —John C. Maxwell
> *The Power of Thinking Big*

The evidence that you might need to do this will involve a situation that has popped into your mind off and on during the reading of this chapter. You might very well have a sinking feeling in your stomach and want to groan. Furthermore, you're beginning to envision yourself actually approaching the other party in love.

Please act on what the Lord is showing you! Maybe you've already tried to verbally make amends with no results and need to apply Matt. 5:43-44. If so, dare to live out love, even in the face of hostility. Send a card or some flowers, bake her some bread or cookies. Do *good* to that person! In doing so, you'll be living Christ. You'll know a freedom you've never known—a freedom to be the salt to an unsaved world and embrace others with love as God has called all of us to do.

Think About It

- Is there anyone to whom the Lord is asking me to apologize?
- Is there anyone I believe owes me an apology and with whom I have therefore not pursued reconciliation?
- Have I allowed any conflicts that I observed to create bitterness in my heart?
- Have I been spiritually stunted by my own conflicts or the conflicts of others?

6
The Cycle of Conflict

∿∿∿∿∿∿∿∿∿∿∿∿∿∿∿∿∿

Thanks be to God, who always leads us in triumphal procession in Christ and through us spreads everywhere the fragrance of the knowledge of him.
—2 Cor. 2:14

I remember the first time I saw a tornado. I was 10, and we were living in Olathe, Kansas, where my father was attending MidAmerica Nazarene University. We had moved to Kansas from east Texas, and at that time east Texas wasn't widely known for tornadoes. But Kansas certainly was!

That night my mother and I had made a quick trip to the grocery store and had arrived back to our third-floor apartment. We weren't home long before the sound of a piercing siren seemed to split the sky. My father had been listening to the radio. His eyes wide, he instructed our family to leave the apartment and head toward the basement.

As I raced to the front door, I stopped in midstride and screamed, "I forgot my gerbil!" My parents gave the nod for me to race back to my room and get my pet.

Clutching the cage, I followed my parents and sister down the three flights of stairs. We rushed past the ground floor to the basement. My father still clutched the transistor radio. Minutes passed. When nothing happened, we crept back up the basement stairs and inched open the door. The wind and rain lashed at the trees and building.

Soon the cacophony of elements stopped. A deathly silence shrouded the city. The sirens shrieked forth once more, and the announcer's voice grew more frantic by the second.

We all four looked upward to see the reason for the weatherman's delirium. A lone cylindrical cloud coiled in a slow spiral like a huge snake. Still clutching my gerbil, I gulped and stared wide-eyed at the monster that looked as if its prime target was the field behind our apartment building. However, the cloud only accomplished three full rotations before a gentle breeze danced across the field. As if God himself expelled a poof of breath upon a tragedy in the making, the spiraling cloud broke up. And I'm certain the mild wind carried upon it the sighs of my parents, who must have been praying as they had never prayed in their lives.

After living in Kansas for a while, my father became the pastor of a church in Arkansas. During the five years we lived there, I never actually *saw* any tornadoes. But I'm certain I heard one or two roaring over our house. I remember tornado drills at school and being rushed home early from school as tornado-producing clouds rolled our way. One day our family was out doing church visitation, and a tornado descended the road we frequently traveled. On our way back home, we stared wide-eyed at a house whose roof had been ripped off.

Eventually our family settled back into east Texas. I met and married my husband, and we settled down amid the Texas hills for a nice, long life together. My husband grew up in east Texas and says he never remembers even hearing of a tornado near his home. After we married 20 years ago, he didn't quite understand my terror of dark clouds and strong wind. "It's just the wind," he would say. But I had seen and heard too much to be comforted by his calmness.

In the scheme of things, tornado alley somehow managed to shift itself and dip across east Texas. In the late 1980s, we started having tornadoes—and I mean *tornadoes*. The first one I remember proved to be about a mile in width. It mowed through the east Texas countryside, decapitating pines, flattening houses, and causing numerous deaths. My husband and I stood outside and listened to the roar as that monster whirled about three miles from our home. Afterward, we drove up to "Lookout Mountain," a scenic roadside park five miles away, to find that the whole park and its lovely trees had been demolished.

After that tornado, east Texas started having tornadoes the way I remembered them in Arkansas. Now, some 15 years later, it seems that almost every time a dark cloud boils in, somebody in east Texas sees a tornado. I even saw one the other day, hanging out of a cloud about half a mile from the highway down which I was driving. In short, my children, now five and seven, are growing up with the same paranoia I experienced about dark clouds.

While some areas of the world amazingly never experience tornadoes, other areas seem to be trapped in a cycle of destructive weather that just won't quit. I believe destructive behavioral patterns are much like those harmful weather patterns. If a woman ever gets trapped in such a negative pattern, she might remain ensnared for life.

The cycle of conflict is one such negative behavioral pattern. Like a horrific tornado, full-blown conflict tears at our own minds as well as the minds of everyone involved. A cycle of conflict can also stop us from building lasting relationships, because each conflict works like a tornado that destroys all the interpersonal bonding we've worked to achieve. Furthermore, continual conflicts repel those who want to focus upon the goodness of God, develop healthy friendships, and live in peace.

According to Jon Johnston, "Difficult people are as rare as air."[1] Every group or organization you're a part of will feature all sorts of difficult people, many of whom are trapped in a cycle of conflict. In my life experience I have observed numerous people, including myself, who at one time or another have fallen into such a cycle. Therefore, it's important to consider the cycle of conflict. By first examining its traits, we can discover the best method of breaking the cycle as well as how to deal with friends who are trapped in such destructive patterns.

> **Hurting people hurt other people. Once you learn this, it's easier to "turn the other cheek."**
> —John C. Maxwell
> *The Power of Thinking Big*

Cycle of Conflict

People in a cycle of conflict—

- live a *lifestyle* of conflict. Instead of having a life of peace with occasional conflicts, these people have a lifestyle of conflict with occasional peace.
- whenever possible drag every person in their sphere into the cycle by (1) discussing conflicts, (2) inciting acquaintances to take sides, (3) encouraging friends to participate in their conflict, (4) stirring up one-on-one conflicts.
- usually focus most conversations on the latest brawl.
- most likely are unaware that they're in a cycle of conflict and therefore deny it.
- always blame the other person and never take responsibility for their own actions.

The Cycle of Conflict

- are not necessarily laypersons only. Sometimes even ministry professionals and leaders are trapped in a cycle of conflict and live from one conflict to the next with church members or with friends who are also ministry professionals. When this is the case, the church most likely will either not grow or will undergo splits, and the ministry professional, firmly in denial, will always blame the church members or other parties. Frequently, spiritual abuse will also occur as part of the cycle of conflict.
- have a childish, "me"-centered attitude and have never fulfilled Eph. 4:1-3, 12-16:

   As a prisoner for the Lord, then, I urge you to live a life worthy of the calling you have received. Be completely humble and gentle; be patient, bearing with one another in love. Make every effort to keep the unity of the Spirit through the bond of peace . . . to prepare God's people for works of service, so that the body of Christ may be built up until we all reach unity in the faith and in the knowledge of the Son of God and become mature, attaining to the whole measure of the fullness of Christ. Then we will no longer be infants [children, NKJV], tossed back and forth by the waves, and blown here and there by every wind of teaching and by the cunning and craftiness of men in their deceitful scheming. Instead, speaking the truth in love, we will in all things grow up into him who is the Head, that is, Christ. From him the whole body, joined and held together by every supporting ligament, grows and builds itself up in love, as each part does its work.

Notice that the above passsage refers to growing up in Christ and therefore ending our activities as infants and/or children. This exhortation is extended within the context of "[making] every effort to keep the unity of the Spirit through the bond of peace" (v. 3). In short, I believe that making effort toward peace comes only when we have divorced ourselves from a childish cycle of conflict.

In observing children at play, you know that it's typical of them, especially siblings, to move from one conflict to the next. In other words, it's natural for children to exist within a cycle of conflict. Sadly, some people grow to adulthood and never break out of this cycle. Often these individuals have for some reason been stunted in their spiritual, mental, or emotional maturity or have chosen to remain in their childhood development level concerning interpersonal relationships.

As already mentioned, I speak from experience. Due to my own severe family of origin issues, I can look back over my 20s and see that I was a young woman who was so devastated that I was essentially emotionally and spiritually stunted at about age 15. Therefore, if you see some of these traits in your own life, I urge you to take heart—there is hope! The following suggestions for breaking the cycle of conflict are proven and effective and have brought about freedom in my life.

If you want to break the cycle of conflict—

- **Identify and admit that you're trapped in an unhealthful behavioral pattern.** Examine the last five years of your life, and honestly determine whether you've lived from one conflict to the next in your friendships or you've generally experienced a lifestyle of peace. Is there a number of strained, broken, or estranged friendships in which you've taken no blame for the break? Denying the problem will only cause havoc in your relationships. Some people have gone to their graves living a cycle of conflict with a past full of shattered friendships.
- **Examine the source.** Two main causes for this cycle ex-

ist. As already mentioned, most people caught in this cycle are living in a childish mentality. Like me, some may be able to point to a horrid experience or a series of experiences that stunted their emotional, mental, or spiritual growth. The second cause involves the sins of the father and/or mother. If one or both of your parents raised you while living a cycle of conflict in front of you, then you might very well be fulfilling Num. 14:18— "The LORD is slow to anger, abounding in love and forgiving sin and rebellion. Yet he does not leave the guilty unpunished; he punishes the children for the sin of the fathers to the third and fourth generation." In my estimation, this does not mean that God will punish me for a sin my father or mother commits without my knowledge. But if my father and/or mother train me in a sinful activity and I as an adult don't choose to break the generational sin, then I'll be held accountable. Some families are entrenched in a cycle of conflict and have been for generations. Some parents simply never matured themselves because of reasons already alluded to and therefore never provided an example of emotional maturity for their children. If your family is cursed with a cycle of conflict, you can choose to break the cycle in your own life. In turn, God will indeed prove himself "slow to anger, abounding in love and forgiving sin and rebellion." He will also give you a new freedom, joy, and lasting power in your friendships. Whatever the cause of the cycle, identifying the source is an important and unavoidable step in breaking this destructive behavioral pattern.

- **Pray for deliverance.** Once the source is identified, commit to *regularly* praying for deliverance. Beseech the Lord to break the chains binding your heart due to the identified source. During your prayer time, allow God to shine His light upon your heart, and write down every negative behavioral pattern He brings to your mind. He very likely will replay numerous past conflicts through your thoughts and remind you of the part you played. Be brave enough to write down what He shows you. After several instances, you'll most likely identify a recurring pattern. For instance, you might find that you live out one of the patterns I exhibited in my early 20s—taking offense because of a tiny issue and then blowing up in an emotional and teary fit. Your list might include a few pattern sequences or even dozens, depending on how entrenched this cycle is in your life. Once you pinpoint your behavioral patterns, begin praying for deliverance from the patterns one by one. Be aware that working through these types of issues takes time. Be prepared to commit 30 minutes to 1 hour at least several days a week, preferably every day, to allow the Lord to purge your heart and life of these destructive patterns. Don't be surprised if His purging involves weeks of struggle, tears, and pain. This type of spiritual growth is never easy, quick, or cheap.

- **Ask God to give you the wisdom to "think on your feet."** Part of breaking the cycle will involve being so in tune with the Lord that you sense His bells of caution if you're about to enter into the negative cycle. At this point it's appropriate and effective to enter into Spirit-led self-talk. For instance, you can facilitate breaking the pattern(s) by being aware when you're on the verge of falling into the cyclical behavior. When you sense that you're reverting to the old patterns, talk to yourself. Say something like *Self, the last time I was involved in a friendship and this subject came up, I fell into a conflict. This might be a good time to take a rest room break and get a grip.* Politely excuse yourself, and while in the rest room pray like crazy for self-control. Remind yourself that you value the friendship more than your need to defend or be right. If breaking away from the setting isn't appropriate, politely change the subject. Or if humor fits your personality type, crack a joke. Any diversion will prove a wise means of steering clear of falling back into the old patterns.

The Cycle of Conflict

- **As the Lord leads, make restitution for your past conflicts.** Lev. 6:1-7 details the Old Testament method for making restitution for some sins. While we are no longer under the old law, this Old Testament concept is still alive today, because a truly repentant person will not rest until everything possible has been done to make peace with others. Prov. 28:13 wisely states, "He who conceals his sins does not prosper, but whoever confesses and renounces them finds mercy." While restitution in no way buys God's forgiveness, the act of saying, "I'm sorry," and making amends is the natural outpouring of a contrite spirit. A woman who stiffly says, "I know God has forgiven me, and I've forgiven her, but I'll never say I'm sorry," has by no means encountered the power of God's forgiveness. The woman who has experienced such a powerful release will in turn freely extend the Lord's love and beg others for forgiveness for any wrongs she has committed. Therefore, a huge element in finding freedom from a sinful cycle involves making restitution because (1) restitution is a natural outpouring of true repentance, and (2) saying, "I'm sorry," when we've been wrong has a way of teaching us not to repeat the pattern. When the Lord started breaking this cycle in my own life, I went through two years of confessing and making amends. Once that two-year purging was complete, I decided that I would rather do my best through God's power to live conflict-free than have to continually grovel about my negative behavior.

- **Expect failures.** As with any negative cycle of behavior, you'll most likely find that you might occasionally revert to the old patterns, especially if you're with a friend or family member who's living a cycle of conflict. The closer you are to complete deliverance, the less frequently you'll fall back into the cycle. When you do fail, throw yourself upon the mercy of the Father, sit at the feet of Jesus, admit your guilt, pray for strength, and make amends as the

Lord leads. Furthermore, I've learned to be on guard around those who exhibit the cycle of conflict. As recovering alcoholics are advised to be on guard when they see someone else drinking alcohol, so those who are delivered from the cycle of conflict should be wise when interacting with others who live a lifestyle of conflict. This statement is in no way a validation for breaking off friendships with those who are in a cycle of conflict. Rather, its purpose is to encourage those struggling with this cycle to forever be cautious when dealing with persons who might prove to be a source of new conflicts.

- **Be aware that you aren't alone.** If in reading through this section you feel as if you've discovered something startling and disturbing about yourself, relax and realize that you're not alone in this cycle of conflict. Once the Lord made me aware of this cycle in my own life and ultimately delivered me, I began to notice the same patterns in the lives of numerous other friends—some Christians, some not. Interestingly enough, many times both parties involved in conflicts can be and often are living a cycle of conflict. I believe this can be the case in many large church brawls that involve numerous parties who once were friends. On a broader scale, often wars erupt due to nations who are living a cycle of conflict. Many people live in such a cycle their whole lives and never seem to be aware of it. But once you dare step through the gateway to freedom, you'll fully understand what Christ meant when He said, "Come to Me, all you who are weary and heavy laden, and I will give you rest. Take My yoke upon you and learn from Me, for I am gentle and lowly in heart; and you will find rest for your souls" (Matt. 11:28-29, NKJV). Indeed, breaking free of the cycle of conflict delivers rest and tranquillity to all our relationships—our friends and family members as well as our business and church companions.

> **Somewhere along the line every Christian woman wishes she had a sister to help her negotiate the twists and turns of life.**
> —Donna Otto
> "Discover the Mentor in You," *Virtue,* July-August 1996

Dealing with Those Who Are Living a Cycle of Conflict

Perhaps you aren't involved in perpetual conflicts, but you recognize the negative pattern in the lives of some of your friends, family members, and/or acquaintances. You might even look back and see times when they actually dragged you into some of their upheavals. Perhaps you even found yourself taking sides between two valued friends or being accused of taking sides, even if you didn't. If you honestly are not living a cycle of conflict but are trying to deal with friends who are, the following suggestions will prove valuable in saving relationships and keeping yourself from being involved in unnecessary discord.

When dealing with friends in a cycle of conflict—

- **"Be wise as serpents and harmless as doves"** (Matt. 10:16, NKJV). While recognizing that the cycle in your friend's life is important, be aware that a wise heart never behaves condescendingly to those who are in the maturing process. Think of yourself as a dove of peace who will minister to a friend in need. If you "think of yourself more highly than you ought" (Rom. 12:3) and look down upon the friend, you will only give her all the more reason to fall into a conflict with you. Also realize that looking down on another person in any situation destroys all chances that you'll minister to the person. Jesus Christ called us to serve one another. Truly living the heart of Christ in our friendships annihilates all traces of condescension. Nevertheless, in light of maintaining Christlike attitudes, be wise to the fact that your friend is living a cycle of conflict, and don't allow yourself to be sucked into that cycle.

- **Listen to and obey the Lord.** This point is pivotal to peacefully coexisting with a person trapped in a cycle of conflict. God is the only one who can see to the very bottom of your friend's heart, and He is the one who will guide you in how to deal with your friend. He might tell you to keep your distance and ask no questions or move in close and prayerfully get to the bottom of an issue. Whatever you do, make certain you irrevocably know the mind of Christ before acting or speaking. This kind of certainty in the Lord comes about only after habitually seeking Him and daily living in the Spirit. Realize that getting your opinions mixed up with God's promptings will almost always result in conflict and dissension. When dealing with a person in a cycle of conflict, many times it's best to live by the following two scriptures: "Set a guard over my mouth, O LORD; keep watch over the door of my lips. Let not my heart be drawn to what is evil, to take part in wicked deeds" (Ps. 141:3-4); "He who holds his tongue is wise" (Prov. 10:19). And if you *do* know beyond doubt that the Lord is calling you to speak, remember to apply Eph. 4:15 and speak the truth in love.

- **Realize that people in a cycle of conflict will always make themselves look faultless while denigrating the other party.** Instead of taking responsibility for their part of the conflict, they have an "It's their fault" mentality. (As already stated, most young children exhibit this behavior.) Therefore, try to steer conversations away from the latest conflict. Rudely refusing to discuss conflicts will only offend your friend. Rather, live out Prov. 13:3—"He who guards his lips guards his life, but he who speaks rashly will come to ruin." Then in a mature fashion, lead the conversation away from interpersonal pitfalls. If by some chance you try but fail to stop a conversational focus upon conflict, do everything in your power to refuse to take sides. The person in a cycle of conflict never sees the latest brawl in a detached manner but rather bends every sequence of events to make himself or herself appear guiltless. No matter what the person tells you about the other party, remember that almost every conflict has three sides—two human sides and the right side. Jumping in on one side will immediately and irrevocably put you at odds with the other person. If at all possible, do your best to maintain neutrality and "make every effort to live in peace with all men" (Heb. 12:14).

- **If a friend has dragged you into a conflict, guard yourself against being involved again.** Realize that the person in a cycle of conflict will repeat the cycle. If you've been dragged into past conflicts, you will most likely be included in future conflicts if you don't consciously choose not to participate. In order to achieve this goal, I have at times stepped away from a group conversation in which a particular conflict was the topic of focus. I have also at times chosen not to receive information about what somebody else was supposed to have said about me. Another tactic that has repeatedly proven successful for me is saying something positive about the other person who is supposed to be involved in the conflict. "Whatever is true, whatever is noble, whatever is right, whatever is pure, whatever is lovely, whatever is admirable—if anything is excellent or praiseworthy—think about such things" (Phil. 4:8).

- **Make amends when appropriate.** Realize that those caught in a cycle of conflict can falsely accuse friends of negative motives or behavior. Sometimes the accusers firmly believe these accusations despite the fact that the accusations are false. Depending upon the severity of their cycle of conflict, these people can do everything from getting angry and turning a cold shoulder to full-blown slander or legal claims. In the most severe circumstances, the innocent party has no recourse but to hire a lawyer for defense. But in cases in which a friend is turning a cold shoulder, often this behavior is a means of manipulation in order to get a friend to beg for forgiveness when the friend is honestly not in the wrong. If someone is attempting to manipulate you in this vein, then (1) search your own heart, (2) allot a significant amount of time to allow God to search your heart, and (3) if you have honestly done nothing, be aware that pursuing this friend might only enable and entrench the cycle. While I am a major proponent of making amends and begging forgiveness, in a few cases the Lord impressed me to simply wait because I had done nothing wrong, and trying to pursue the friend would only cause a blowup—which is exactly what people in a cycle of conflict thrive upon. Other times the Lord has impressed me to send a card of appreciation or a small friendship gift and never mention the friend's negative behavior. In most of these cases I have found that the friend will soon move on to another conflict and forget why she was even mad at me in the first place. Be open to the leading of the Holy Spirit.

- **Don't automatically break the friendship.** Many people in church and out are living a cycle of conflict. As tornadoes vary in severity, some cycles of conflict are mild while others are habitually devastating. If you break off a friendship with every person you suspect is involved in any form of these unhealthful patterns, you might lose contact with some of your most delightful acquaintances. Just because a woman is in a cycle of conflict doesn't mean that she has nothing to offer as a friend. Nor does it mean that she doesn't *need* a friend. Sometimes those who are living in conflict are the most emotionally needy. Instead of breaking off the friendship, live Jesus Christ; allow the Lord to love and minister to that friend through you. Eventually, you just might be the one to show her the pathway to freedom. "You will know the truth, and the truth will set you free" (John 8:32).

- **"Dust your feet" of the relationship only if God leads.** In Matt. 10 Jesus told His disciples, "Whatever town or village you enter, search for some worthy person there and stay at his house until you leave. As you enter the home, give it your greeting. If the home is deserving, let your peace rest on it; if it is not, let your peace return to you. If anyone will not welcome you or listen to your words, shake the dust off your feet when you leave that home or town. . . . I am sending you out like sheep among wolves" (vv. 11-14, 16). Realize that some people are trapped in sinful cycles and will refuse to hear the voice of the Lord. God himself knows who these people are, and He will direct you if you should back off and permanently keep a safe distance. As indicated in the previous point, I don't make a habit of recommending that people break off friendships. However, there are a rare few people out there who are so entrenched in their blindness that they will coldly, purposefully, and habitually hurt those who have repeatedly offered kindness upon kindness. Some of these people are actually church members. In all my own interpersonal relationships, I've encountered only a handful of people whom the Lord has impressed upon me to keep a safe distance from or allow the relationship to dissolve. However, I absolutely never take this course of action unless I'm certain, beyond all doubt, of this divine direction.

- **Use this book as a ministry tool.** Either work through the book together as a friendship team, or initiate a group study and naturally discuss this chapter as it occurs.

- **Realize that only God can change hearts.** If a friend won't listen to God, she won't listen to you. Anytime someone expresses a negative attitude that I'm required to respond to, I'm learning to simply ask how long that person prayed about the opinion. I then ask if she would be willing to commit 30-40 minutes in prayer about the issue. If she agrees, then I rely on the Lord to show her the truth. Often what occurs after such a season of prayer is a softening of the spirit and an apology, if necessary. I'm learning that if a woman won't be still before God and listen to His voice, then she certainly won't listen to me. Once you really understand this, it frees you from needing to defend yourself and from the desire to change others. Only God can change a woman's heart, and only if she lets Him.

> **Consider how hard it is to change yourself, and you'll understand what little chance you have of trying to change others.**
> —Jacob M. Braude

Think About It

- Am I trapped in a cycle of conflict?
- Do I have friends who are involved in a cycle of conflict?
- Have I been dragged into discord by someone in a cycle of conflict?
- Am I fully equipped to continue to be friends with those in a cycle of conflict while avoiding their strife?

7
Forgiving Friends

∿∿∿∿∿∿∿∿∿∿∿∿∿∿∿∿∿∿∿∿∿∿

If you forgive men when they sin against you, your heavenly Father will also forgive you. But if you do not forgive men their sins, your Father will not forgive your sins.
—Matt. 6:14-15

The dogs were barking when I turned off my vacuum cleaner. I knew before I even opened the front door that the way they were yelping meant only one thing—*snake!* My gray mutt, Molly, and black chow, Pepper, were barking for all they were worth with their noses pointed right into one of my flower beds. Then Molly jerked away from the irises and lilies, and something long and black lunged toward her, then recoiled into the flowers.

I stood in the doorway, chills dancing up and down my spine, and wondered what to do. Actually, when you live out in the country, a snake in the afternoon isn't so peculiar. However, this time was different. I was home by myself. All the time we lived at that house, every snake had conveniently shown up when my husband, Daniel, was home.

After two hard swallows, I crept toward the flower bed. I wanted to get close enough to see what kind of snake it was but not so close that it could see what kind of person *I* was.

The dogs continued their steady onslaught of barking, and my insides were coiled up as tightly as the four-foot, black-taupe snake in the flower bed. I peered at it from a safe five feet away, took a deep breath of the east Texas piney air, and tried to calm myself enough to determine the creature's fate.

The serpent didn't look all that harmful. Even though it was rather large, it still didn't appear to be anything more than a chicken snake or a king snake or another variety of nonpoisonous serpent prevalent in Texas.

I could just leave it in hopes it'll crawl away, I mused. But the look in my yapping dogs' eyes told me they would bark at the thing until their tongues fell out. I knew the snake wouldn't get away with those two around.

The serpent flung itself at Pepper, stretching its long body as far as it could. Pepper jumped away, the hair prickling on the back of his neck—and mine.

I guess I could kill it, I thought. But I hated to. It might not be poisonous, and snakes *do* have their place in nature. I'm a nature person and hate to disturb what God has set in balance. But when nature is "balancing" in my yard, that's a different matter!

I chewed my lip and rubbed the hair standing out on my arms. What if the thing tried to bite me while I was killing it? How *would* I kill it? With a shovel or—I remembered my husband's revolver. *I could use that,* I thought.

But I didn't want to. All I wanted to do was go back in the house, lock the door, and hope the thing went away. That is, if it weren't poisonous.

But *what if* it were poisonous? After all, I could see some sort of taupish-gray pattern on its back. Did chicken snakes have that pattern?

Several minutes passed, and now my dogs were barking and looking at me as if they expected me to take action. I knew I had to. As if I were John Wayne himself riding out to face the enemy, I thought, *Sometimes you just do what you gotta do.*

Forgiving Friends

I won't go into the gory details of the serpent slaughter. But after a dual effort of my husband's gun and a shovel, I managed to remove the thing from my flower bed.

Yet I did notice something very intriguing before I tossed the creature to its final resting-place across the road. The inside of its mouth was white—like cotton.

After dumping the lifeless body in the prickly, ankle-deep grass, I stared at the form for a minute. Could it be? Nah, not a water moccasin. It had to be nonpoisonous.

Or was it? Who cared now? The ordeal was over, and my two dogs were satisfied.

When Daniel arrived home, I wanted him to confirm my nonpoisonous diagnosis. Upon viewing the corpse, however, Daniel assured me that I had murdered a very poisonous water moccasin.

I swallowed hard. "And to think I almost didn't kill it."

"I know it took a lot of guts, but I'm glad you did. If that thing had bitten one of us . . ."

"Point taken."

I was reminded of Adam and Eve in the garden. They didn't think their serpent was very poisonous either. I also thought of how Christians so often follow Adam and Eve's example. We rationalize, *It's just a little sin—just one, innocuous wrong attitude.* And we go along, leaving deadly serpents in our lives when God wants us to kill them on the spot.

Often these "serpents" slither into the deepest recesses of our hearts in the form of unforgiveness and resentment—despite the fact that we're in church every Sunday. From the outside, no one would ever suspect that we're harboring such wicked spiritual snakes. But when we're alone with God, He might regularly put His finger on the unforgiveness we have against a friend, unforgiveness we've refused to release to Him.

After a conflict, I believe that one of the main things that keeps friends separated is unforgiveness. Usually the closer the friends have been, the more bitter the unforgiveness. It can also be like a fungus that gnaws at a tree from the inside out. While on the outside the tree might very well look great, the inside is hollow and black. None of us is free of the need to be forgiven. Therefore, we have no right to harbor unforgiveness toward a friend or acquaintance—no matter how deep the betrayal.

This is in no way a subtle way for me to say, "Get over it." I've been through too much in life to ever take that approach. However, true forgiveness will never happen until we first realize that we have no "holy license" to cling to resentment. But even within that context, I also believe that forgiveness can and does come in the form of a process that might happen over a period of time. Indeed, forgiveness can be compared to an onion that must be peeled one layer at a time. God is able and willing to begin that process and bring complete healing and restoration to your soul and your friendships if you're willing.

Therefore, the heart of this chapter is dedicated to "the pathway of forgiveness." Far from being a series of abstract shoulds and should nots, the following path represents my own struggles with forgiveness and what I've learned in order to find freedom from the past.

> **I'm amazed at how quickly He forgot**
> **All the sin and the wrong I had brought**
> **To the cross of Calvary**
> **When His blood was shed for me.**
> **I'm amazed that it covers every sin.**
> **Yes, I'm amazed at how quickly He forgot.**
> —Terry Toler

Forgiving Friends

The Pathway of Forgiveness

Step One: **Pray that God will enable you to forgive.**

Scripture: "Forgive us our debts, as we also have forgiven our debtors" (Matt. 6:12). "For if you forgive men when they sin against you, your heavenly Father will also forgive you. But if you do not forgive men their sins, your Father will not forgive your sins" (vv. 14-15).

This prayer must stem from a heart that really wants to be enabled to forgive. A halfhearted prayer of *Lord, please help me to forgive, but let me rip out her heart first* won't avail anything. While honesty with God is important, we still need to desire to do what's right. Frankly, I think much of the desires of our hearts are bound up in our desires for the Lord. When our ultimate goal in life is to please Him, then we focus not on obeying the sinful nature but on what His Word urges. We understand that He is love and all that He asks of us is for our good because He loves us.

Practical Steps. The following prayers will help you in your journey to forgiveness.

1. If you truly cannot find a desire to forgive, then start right there: *Lord, I really want to do something horrible to this person, so I need You to give me the desire to forgive.* However, don't use this prayer as an excuse not to forgive. For instance, thinking, *I don't feel like forgiving, so God doesn't expect me to* is not in His will. However, if you mean this prayer, He'll be faithful to fulfill your desires.

2. Be honest: *Lord, You know I'm struggling with wanting to retaliate, but my desire is more to do what You want than what my flesh insists. Help!*

3. *Lord, remind me that You died for this person just as You died for me. Give me the depth of love that freely extends forgiveness.*

Step Two: **Ask the Lord to show you reality.**

Scripture: "King Xerxes asked Queen Esther, 'Who is he? Where is the man who has dared to do such a thing?' Esther said, 'The adversary and the enemy is this vile Haman.' Then Haman was terrified before the king and queen. The king got up in a rage, left his wine and went out into the palace garden. But Haman, realizing that the king had already decided his fate, stayed behind to beg Queen Esther for his life" (Esther 7:5-7).

"Do not be deceived: God cannot be mocked. A man reaps what he sows. The one who sows to please his sinful nature, from that nature will reap destruction; the one who sows to please the Spirit, from the Spirit will reap eternal life" (Gal. 6:7-8).

"All have sinned and fall short of the glory of God" (Rom. 3:23).

"Search me, O God, and know my heart; test me and know my anxious thoughts. See if there is any offensive way in me, and lead me in the way everlasting" (Ps. 139:23-24).

First, the story of Haman's plot against the Jews is an excellent example of a murderer whose heart was dark with the sin of pride. However, Queen Esther turned the tables on him and revealed his sin. Haman's reaction shows exactly where every perpetrator eventually lands—a prisoner of desperation because of sin. Rest assured: all sin leads to torment and despair. Either God will make the person miserable with conviction, or, if the person's conscience is seared and he or she doesn't ask forgiveness, punishment will come in the afterlife. Also consider that living a lifestyle of harming others only heaps more heartache and turmoil onto the perpetrator with every evil act. In other words, people who harm others will be in turn harmed—either by the very spiritual torment their acts inflict or by the retaliation of other sinful human beings. This puts the person who harmed you in a different light, because you'll eventually see a pathetic soul living a defeated life and going out to eternal darkness without God. If this person has been a close friend, the heartache will be all the more intense.

Second, in order to maintain an unforgiving spirit, a woman must believe that she's something that she isn't—a person above the possibility of sin. Usually an unforgiving spirit is accompanied by a person saying something like "I would never . . ." and the implication is that the bitter person is above the possibility of sin or of that particular type of sin. In reality, we all must ask the Lord to show us if there's any wicked way in us. In order to follow Christ, we all must come to a point of asking Him to forgive us of our sins. Once we get a picture of ourselves at the foot of the Cross, holding the hammer in our hands, with Jesus' blood dripping onto us, then we realize on a very deep level that we have no right to hold a grudge against another human being. "All have [indeed] sinned and fall short of the glory of God" (Rom. 3:23). That includes you and me. Therefore, in order to hold on to an unforgiving spirit, a woman must be blinded to the fact that she is as deeply in need of forgiveness as the one who inflicted the harm. When we pretend that we don't need forgiveness, we become self-righteous and no longer find our righteousness in Christ.

Practical Steps:

1. Pray that the Lord will show you the person you need to forgive as He sees her—a desperate soul He died for and in need of His love.

2. Remember that many people who harm others have themselves been very deeply wounded in the past. Ask God to show you their bleeding hearts.

3. Pray that the Lord will give you a clear and honest view of yourself without Him and that He will show you your desperate need of His forgiveness.

4. Pray that the Lord will show you what sins you might have committed against your friends if you had been without Him in your life.

5. Realize that you might very well shy away from implementing these steps. Human beings rarely enjoy having the light of God shine into the crevices of their souls to this level. *But true forgiveness for others never occurs until we have encountered the truth of our own desperate need of forgiveness.*

Step Three: As much as lies within you, *calmly* and *honestly* share your pain with the person who injured you.

Scripture: "*Speaking the truth in love*, we will in all things grow up into him who is the Head, that is, Christ. From him the whole body, joined and held together by every supporting ligament, grows and builds itself up in love, as each part does its work" (Eph. 4:15-16, emphasis added).

As already discussed in chapter 5, true peace is never achieved by sweeping issues under the rug. But neither is it achieved by blasting a friend with an uncontrolled explosion of our emotions and disillusionment. There's no hope for ever moving past the strain of the past without heavy doses of honesty and wisdom along with self-control. Therefore, solid friendships can be reformed and mended when the shadows of an unresolved conflict are dealt with honestly and are bathed in prayer.

Practical Steps. Talking about tough issues is not easy and takes plenty of courage. The following suggestions will help you in your journey. Remember: if multiple issues are involved, take one issue at a time—unless several are interrelated—as the Lord brings them to your mind during your prayer life.

1. Set an appointment to talk about the problem. Make sure you will have time and privacy. Or, if you choose an

unplanned discussion, use discretion regarding privacy and time.

2. Don't accuse and hurl insults, but also don't avoid the issues.

3. If appropriate, ask your friend to pray with you before you begin the discussion.

4. Realize that tears might be inevitable.

5. Once the issue has been discussed, don't keep bringing it up. Let it go.

6. Understand that the more numerous the unresolved issues, the longer it will take to work through them. In other words, if one friendship has suffered 8 to 10 upheavals, then realize that working through them might take several months or years, depending on the severity of the issues. By the same token, if you're dealing with only 1 issue, then expect a more speedy resolution.

7. Don't sermonize or preach or evaluate your friend's spiritual condition. Stick to the topic at hand.

8. If your friend expresses no remorse, then commit the issue and your friend to daily prayer. Frankly, a *need* to be begged for forgiveness is a sign that true forgiveness has not occurred. While someone asking our forgiveness can hasten the process and certainly facilitate reconciliation, true forgiveness does not hinge upon the perpetrator's remorse. True forgiveness stems from God's grace, mercy, and power. This depth of supernatural forgiveness is available from the Lord, even in the face of disdain from the offending party.

Step Four: **Commit to repeated mental forgiveness.**

Scripture: "Then Peter came to Him and said, 'Lord, how often shall my brother sin against me, and I forgive him? Up to seven times?' Jesus said to him, 'I do not say to you, up to seven times, but up to seventy times seven'" (Matt. 18:21-22, NKJV).

Traditionally this passage is interpreted to mean that if someone sins against us 490 times (or 77 times, NIV), then we should forgive that person each and every time. In other words, our forgiveness should be infinite—no matter how many times that person sins against us. However, allow me to offer a slightly different approach. I think perhaps if someone sins against us, the negative incident will come back to us over and over again—perhaps 490 times—even after we make a decision to forgive. Frankly, I have experienced this very thing myself—even after trusting the Lord to enable me to forgive someone.

Practical Steps. Every time you think of the wrong done to you, "Take captive every thought to make it obedient to Christ" (2 Cor. 10:5).

1. Firmly tell yourself that you've forgiven the person and that it's under the blood of Jesus. If you dwell on the sin, you'll only be tempted to fall back into bitterness.

2. If at all possible, think positive thoughts about that person. For instance, you might think, *My friend is a great singer* or *She's always cheered me with her laughter* or *She's the greatest shopping mate in the world.*

3. Retrain yourself to react in love rather than anger. When the anger begins, go back to Step One above, and then release that anger to the Lord and ask Him to replace it with joy and love. According to Les Parrott,

> Plenty of research now shows that "ventilation" techniques only reduce one's control against anger and encourage more frequent and aggressive forms of the behavior. When we practice letting angry feelings out, we become less able to control them the next time. Rather than "ventilating" the emotion and getting rid of it, we find it returns more frequently. And, like a muscle that we exercise over and over again, those feelings we "exercise" become stronger too.[1]

Forgiving Friends

Gary Smalley writes, "One major reason why forgiveness is so necessary is that anger blocks the working of God's spirit."[2]

Step Five: Ask the Lord to give you a spirit of forgiveness.

Scripture: "When they came to the place called the Skull, there they crucified him, along with the criminals—one on his right, the other on his left. Jesus said, 'Father, forgive them, for they do not know what they are doing'" (Luke 23:33-34).

As already mentioned in chapter 5, if we're to live Christ, we must adopt a spirit of forgiveness. A spirit of forgiveness says that there's nothing a person can do to me that I won't forgive. This type of spirit is from God himself and is the evidence that we have the mind of Christ (1 Cor. 2:16). Jesus Christ exemplified the spirit of forgiveness when He died on the Cross. He forgave not only past and present sins committed against Him but all future sins as well.

A spirit of forgiveness revolutionizes every friendship, because it breeds security. I'm not going to pretend that if one of my friends really mistreated me, I wouldn't struggle. I would. The pain would be great, and the journey to healing would not be overnight. But I'm committed that Christ's spirit of forgiveness in me would prevail.

Practical Steps.

1. Pray not only that you can forgive the specific conflicts that are trapping you in bitterness but also for a spirit of forgiveness that will empower you to repeatedly forgive as future situations arise.

2. Ask a friend or your spouse to pray that you'll adopt a spirit of forgiveness.

3. Pray that your friend will adopt a spirit of forgiveness.

4. Pray together as friends that the Lord will immerse

you in His forgiveness—together, for each other, for the past, and for anything that might arise in the future.

5. Realize that a spirit of forgiveness can be rare—even around the church. As already stated in chapter 5, a spirit of forgiveness is impossible in our human strength. Therefore, many people never experience it because they rely upon themselves to orchestrate such a spirit. However, when we truly abandon ourselves to Christ and to His heart and beseech Him for such a spirit, the inevitable result is an outpouring of His love and forgiveness upon all our friends.

> **Forgiveness is the fragrance the violet sheds on the heel that has crushed it.**
> —Mark Twain

Think About It

- Am I harboring unforgiveness against a friend?
- Is a friend harboring unforgiveness against me?
- Do I truly see myself as undeserving of Christ's forgiveness?
- Am I committed to adopting a spirit of forgiveness for all the wrong committed against me and all the wrong that will be committed against me in the future?

8
The River of Friendship

There is a river whose streams make glad the city of God, the holy place where the Most High dwells.
—Ps. 46:4

Some of my earliest memories include holding a cane pole over an east Texas pier and the afternoons spent in a boat with my dad. During my childhood my parents enjoyed a wide network of friends, and one of the things my family loved to do with friends and family was fishing.

On one particular outing, my parents invited my mother's brother and his wife and kids. That was great with all us cousins, because if the fish weren't biting, we could play in the sand and water. Little did we know that our parents would provide a scene much more amusing than any of us could produce.

This happened back when wigs were popular, and every lady who wanted to be "with it" wore one. Aunt Betty was one of the "with it" ladies. Mama was about to unwittingly relieve her sister-in-law of that status.

Mama stood near the lake and carefully placed the bait on her cane pole's fishing line. Next, she found the perfect place to cast her line. Not realizing that my aunt was directly behind her, she extended the cane pole behind her and prepared to thrust it forward. But she had snagged her hook on something. Assuming that "something" was a bush or tree limb, she tugged with all her might. Finally the hook came free. But much to her surprise, Mama had already made a catch: a fluffy blond wig dangled at the end of her fishing line. The hair landed with a graceful plop in the lake, right where Mama had been aiming.

Imagine a turtle without its shell. That's about what a lady without her wig looks like. To successfully wear a wig, you have to slick down all your hair until you look bald. Aunt Betty now sported the bald look.

Well, we all went into hysterics. Amazingly, Aunt Betty took the whole thing in stride, and no lasting harm was done—unless you count nearly passing out from laughing.

> **Jesus is my best friend. At times I have failed people. At times people have failed me. Jesus never fails.**
> —John C. Maxwell
> *The Power of Thinking*

Sometimes in our efforts at friendship we might be like my mother and her attempts to fish. We start out with good motives and skills. After all, my mother was skilled in solid fishing techniques. We might even memorize all sorts of concepts and be ready to put them into practice. But somehow in our human failings we still can't seem to succeed. Our efforts at kindness might be misunderstood. Our attempts to speak words of wisdom can be misinterpreted. Eventually, our very labor of love might result in some interpersonal catastrophe that's far less humorous than Aunt Betty's wig flying through the air.

My purpose in writing this book is to motivate and equip readers to embrace the world in friendship. By this point I hope you're inspired and ready to begin your journey. However, I must be candid. You'll find your success limited unless you base every attempt at friendship upon the *river of friendship*. For the river of friendship is a source of love that flows straight from the heart of our Heavenly Father.

> *What a Friend we have in Jesus,*
> *All our sins and griefs to bear!*
> *What a privilege to carry*
> *Ev'rything to God in prayer!*
> *O what peace we often forfeit,*
> *O what needless pain we bear,*
> *All because we do not carry*
> *Everything to God in prayer!*
>
> *Have we trials and temptations?*
> *Is there trouble anywhere?*
> *We should never be discouraged;*
> *Take it to the Lord in prayer.*
> *Can we find a friend so faithful*
> *Who will all our sorrows share?*
> *Jesus knows our ev'ry weakness;*
> *Take it to the Lord in prayer.*
>
> *Are we weak and heavy laden,*
> *Cumbered with a load of care?*
> *Precious Savior, still our Refuge!*
> *Take it to the Lord in prayer.*
> *Do thy friends despise, forsake thee?*
> *Take it to the Lord in prayer.*

In His arms He'll take and shield thee;
Thou wilt find a solace there.
—Joseph M. Scriven

The Most Important Friendship of All

It's a mistake to look to a friend or even a spouse to be our everything. Our relationship with God—and only this relationship—can fill that unexplainable void in our souls. Expecting another human being to fulfill this void sets us up for failed relationships. No human being can be our reason for living—despite the contemporary songs that state otherwise. Often we realize in our marriages that our husbands aren't fulfilling all our needs, and we look to friends to fill the gaps. The problem is that soon we sense that even close friendships with other women can't fill the void deep within our souls.

I travel and speak all over North America. At times I'm interviewed on national television and radio. Often people call in to the show with questions or consult me at retreats and conferences about problems relating to whatever subject I'm speaking on or discussing. When people approach me with their various problems, one of the key questions I always ask is: *How much time are you spending with the Lord?* More likely than not, the answer is that the person—either young or old—isn't committing a regular *chunk* of time to simply being still and knowing that He is God.

Despite the fact that churches are full of women who sing in the choir, serve on boards, and head up various ministries, there seems to be an anemia among women in the amount of time in which they're encountering Jesus Christ. Indeed, people often ask other people about their problems before they even think to ask the Lord. I do believe that solid Christian opinion can offer wisdom and that the Lord can speak to us through the insights of others. After all, I do write books for that purpose. However, no human being can ever guide us the way our Lord can guide us. *He* is the one who knows all our problems. *He* is the one who sees our lives and the lives of those about whom we are concerned. *He* is the one who died on the Cross so that we could experience deep, divine friendships that never end. *He* is the one whose heart is broken when we choose not to make Him our best friend of all. Nevertheless, when I ask women, "Are you spending chunks of time with the Lord?" more often than not, the answer is "no."

Sadly, many people never understand that this lack of time spent in the presence of Jesus is the core reason for many of their problems in their friendships, their marriages, and their lack of peace. When we plunge the depths of the most important friendship of all—our friendship with Jesus Christ—we stop forcing unhealthful expectations upon ourselves and others. While we're all called to be Christlike, no one—*absolutely no one*—can fill the place of the Lord in our lives. Indeed, true intimacy with others begins when we dare to develop intimacy with Christ.

The richest friendships start with Christ.

Chunks Needed

I don't know about you, but I *love* chocolate! My love affair with chocolate didn't begin until my early 30s, but it soon exploded into an attachment that's far from waning. I think most healthy women love the dark, rich stuff. I have known some who I believe might trade their most precious possession for a box of Hershey bars. I myself would walk 50 miles for a scoop of German chocolate ice cream! Of course, the Lord knows all this and often fulfills Ps. 37:4

and gives us the desires of our hearts. This divine gift from chocolate heaven is evident at most women's ministries events I've attended, because at some point there's a chocolate dessert in the scheme of things.

The good thing about chocolate is that it glides down the throat smooth as silk and makes the eyes roll in ecstasy. The bad thing about chocolate is that it's full of calories. The bigger the chunks, the higher the calories. The higher the calories, the greater the cellulite. Right now my cellulite supply is thriving! I live for the time when I can daily eat big ol' fat, warm, oozy chocolate chip cookies until I swoon with pleasure. Now *that* would be heaven! I'm almost certain that when the Bible talks about heaven having streets of gold, the Greek word used for "gold" *really* means chocolate!

Seriously, I'm not on some insane chocolate binge. Although I do enjoy indulging from time to time, I've learned not to indulge too much. I've about decided that the average chunk of chocolate has the same calorie count as six hamburgers, two orders of greasy onion rings, and a gallon of ice cream. Therefore, I've learned to curb my cravings.

> **Praise the LORD, O my soul; all my inmost being, praise his holy name. Praise the LORD, O my soul, and forget not all his benefits—who forgives all your sins and heals all your diseases, who redeems your life from the pit and crowns you with love and compassion, who satisfies your desires with good things so that your youth is renewed like the eagle's.**
> —Ps. 103:1-5

There's another craving that most women have. It's deep in the bottom of their souls—a spiritual craving for honest, intimate friendship. This intimacy is quenched only when we dare to consume a high-calorie "spiritual diet." While consuming mounds of high-calorie chocolate chunks might not be healthful physically, consuming a high-calorie "spiritual diet" is about the most healthful spiritual thing we can do. Such a spiritual diet consists of regularly devouring *chunks* of time in the presence of Christ.

Daring to Encounter Him

I have found that many people struggle with developing deep friendships with Christ because they believe that prayer is essentially *talking* to God. Certainly Scripture admonishes, "Do not be anxious about anything, but in everything, by prayer and petition, with thanksgiving, present your requests to God" (Phil. 4:6). Therefore, *talking to* God is a highly important part of prayer. But let's face it—you can pray for a whole league of people and their problems in about 5 to 15 minutes, depending on the length of your list. After that, most women shrug and say, "OK—I've had my prayer time," when in reality they barely got started.

Another important element in prayer is to *praise* the Lord for His holiness, His love, His friendship: "Praise the LORD, O my soul; all my inmost being, praise his holy name" (Ps. 103:1). Thanking the Lord is just as crucial to prayer life. "Let us come before him with thanksgiving and extol him with music and song" (95:2). Nevertheless, you can spend about 5 minutes speaking your thanks and praises and find that you've covered a whole host of His mighty works. Once again, people who stop praying at this point are only at the beginning of the depths that the Lord longs us to share with Him.

I am convinced that the most important element in prayer begins when we fall silent, grow still, listen in the deepest recesses of our hearts for His quiet voice, and ultimately soak up the presence of our dearest friend. There are days when I sit and simply know Him for an hour at a time. I plug in my worship music, get comfortable, close my eyes, and simply bask in His presence. I'm looking forward to the time when my schedule allows me to be still for two to three hours a day.

Understand that I didn't start out with hours at a time. I started this journey with committing about 15 minutes a day. Eventually I found that the 15 minutes just wasn't enough. I longed for more. So I stretched to 30 or 40 minutes a day. Soon I found myself having to tear myself away at an hour. Just as rosebuds gradually unfold into a fragrant bloom, so your prayer time will blossom as you stay on your journey.

Furthermore, understand that I'm not trying to pour you into the mold of my methods. Instead of *listening* to music, I often find my husband *singing* music. Perhaps you're a pianist, and playing is an act of worship for you. You might not be a great music lover. In that case, your quiet time with God will *not* involve music. You might prefer basking in the morning sun near your garden, sitting in your hot tub at night, or lying in the middle of your bed at midday. You might enjoying gazing out a window, while others hear the Lord better with their eyes closed.

> **How precious to me are your thoughts, O God!
> How vast is the sum of them! Were I to count them,
> they would outnumber the grains of sand.
> When I awake, I am still with you.**
> —Ps. 139:17-18

The posture, position, time of day, or method is not the issue. The issue is being *alone* with God and being *still enough* and *free enough from distractions* to focus solely upon Him and His thoughts. During the time that my children

The River of Friendship

were smaller and still getting up in the middle of the night, there were times when this quiet time fell between 2 and 3 A.M. for me. Believe me—God is *longing* to have an intimate friendship with *you*. And He's thrilled when you take the time to bask in His *river of friendship*.

During my journey of being still before the Lord, I began to notice that my mind would wander. My brain races with the best of them, and when my thoughts would begin to wander to the fabric of my life—my friends, family, writing, speaking, and church life—I initially thought, *Bad me!* and attempted to rein my wayward mind back to the task of thinking spiritual thoughts.

I had chastised myself only a few times when the Lord broke into my thoughts and showed me that it was perfectly fine for me to ponder my life in His presence. After all, He is a rational God who cares about every detail of my existence. For instance, if I have a concern with my children, He has shown me that I should actually ponder the problem while being still before Him. If there's an area of injury in my life, He'll take my hand as I mentally walk through the incident that's causing me pain. Through the very act of silently and reverently considering the issue, I have found a river of healing that never runs dry. When I'm trying to decide how to handle a touchy situation with a friend, the Lord has been faithful to teach me how to allow the mind of Christ to work in *my mind*. Without doubt, those who wait upon the Lord and are open to His leading can indeed "have the mind of Christ" (1 Cor. 2:16). More often than not, this act of waiting before the Lord will give me heavenly direction and wisdom in dealing with the tiniest details of my life as well as in structuring my books and preparing my spoken messages. This chunk of time with the Lord is also the reason I'm free—truly free—to befriend anyone He calls me to befriend.

Because of my firm commitment to this "high-calorie" spiritual experience, I've enjoyed a stability and confidence that floods every corridor of my existence. Indeed, a *river of friendship* flows from the throne of God, floods my soul with His love, and empowers me to *want* to befriend people who I know have scorned me. Yes, I'm human. And yes, when someone does something hurtful to me, I'm deeply affected. But after I wipe away the tears and take a deep breath, I always come back to the *river of friendship*, where God himself floods me with His love, heals my woundedness, and renews me to love that person anyway.

> **I have come to believe that the majority of Christians are famishing for the very thing they proclaim as truth but themselves are not feasting upon.**
> —Debra White Smith

Understand that there's absolutely no substitute for being still before the Lord. None. Realize that you'll not develop a deep, lasting intimacy with Him unless you begin the journey of being still and knowing that He is God. Therefore, every friendship and relationship you develop will be only as deep as your relationship with Jesus Christ. How much time are you spending in the healing waters of this heavenly *river of friendship?*

> **Are you struggling with how to be a golden friend?**
> "Be still, and know that I am God" (Ps. 46:10).
>
> **Do you doubt that you can ever enjoy the ministry of friendship?**
> "Be still, and know that I am God" (Ps. 46:10).
>
> **Are you trapped in the fear of intimacy?**
> "Be still, and know that I am God" (Ps. 46:10).

The River of Friendship

Is legalism prohibiting you from developing friendships?
"Be still, and know that I am God" (Ps. 46:10).

Do you struggle with conflict?
"Be still, and know that I am God" (Ps. 46:10).

Are you craving a spirit of forgiveness?
"Be still, and know that I am God" (Ps. 46:10).

Are you so devastated from what life has dealt you that you need a miracle before you can embrace anyone in friendship?
"Be still, and know that I am God" (Ps. 46:10).

Think About It

- Am I trying to develop friendships in my own power or through the power of Jesus Christ?
- Do I expect human relationships to fill the void in my soul that only Christ can fill?
- Am I spending chunks of time each week in the presence of the Lord?
- Do I approach prayer as primarily talking to God or *listening to* God and *absorbing* His presence?
- Have I ever taken the time to ponder my problems, family, and friendships in the presence of the Lord?
- Am I allowing wounds from my past to prohibit me from intimacy with God and intimacy with others?

Notes

Chapter 1
1. Wesley D. Tracy et al., *The Upward Call: Spiritual Formation and the Holy Life* (Kansas City: Beacon Hill Press of Kansas City, 1994), 223.
2. Joyce Meyer, *Me and My Big Mouth: Your Answer Is Right Under Your Nose* (Tulsa, Okla.: Harrison House, 1997), 169-70.
3. Mother Teresa, *A Simple Path*, comp. Lucinda Vardney (New York: Ballantine, 1995), 85.
4. Tim Hansel, *You Gotta Keep Dancin'* (Elgin, Ill.: David C. Cook, 1985), 113.
5. John Maxwell, *The Power of Thinking Big* (Tulsa, Okla.: River Oak Publishing, 2001), 58.
6. Becky Freeman, *Real Magnolias* (Nashville: Thomas Nelson, 1999), 137.
7. Malcolm Muggeridge, *Something Beautiful for God* (San Francisco: Harper and Row, 1971), 118.

Chapter 2
1. Tracy et al., *The Upward Call*, 221.

Chapter 3
1. C. S. Lewis, *The Four Loves*, quoted in Elisa Morgan, "Friendmaking," *Focal Point* (Denver Conservative Baptist Seminary, n.d.), n.p.
2. Donna Partow, *Walking in Total God-Confidence* (Minneapolis: Bethany House, 1999), 253.

Chapter 4
1. Joyce Meyer, *How to Succeed at Being Yourself: Finding the Confidence to Fulfill Your Destiny* (Tulsa, Okla.: Harrison House, 1999), 213.
2. See my book *Romancing Your Husband* (Eugene, Oreg.: Harvest House Publishers, 2001) for a balanced, love-based view of marriage.
3. Tracy et al., 74.
4. Gary Smalley, *Love Is a Decision* (Dallas: Word, 1989), 39.

Chapter 5
1. Smalley, *Love Is a Decision*, 90.

Chapter 6
1. Jon Johnston, *Walls or Bridges: How to Build Relationships That Glorify God* (Grand Rapids: Baker Book House, 1988), 115.

Chapter 7

1. Les Parrott and Leslie Parrott, *Like a Kiss on the Lips* (Grand Rapids: Zondervan Publishing House, 1997), 69-70.

2. Smalley, *Love Is a Decision*, 91.